P9-DFF-313

A LOAD OF HOOEY

A LOAD
OF HOOEY

A Collection of New Short Humor Fiction

BOB
ODENKIRK

INCLUDES SELECTIONS FROM
Famous Quotations—Unabridged

MᴄSWEENEY'S
SAN FRANCISCO

ABOUT THE AUTHOR

*Bob Odenkirk is stuck under a cat holding
someone's wine and a stinky old pipe.*

McSWEENEY'S
SAN FRANCISCO

Copyright © 2014 Bob Odenkirk

Cover illustration by Tony Millionaire.

All rights reserved, including right of reproduction in whole
or in part, in any form.

McSweeney's and colophon are registered trademarks
of McSweeney's, a privately held company with wildly
fluctuating resources.

ISBN: 978-1-938073-88-5

10 9 8 7 6 5 4 3 2

www.mcsweeneys.net

THE ODENKIRK MEMORIAL LIBRARY

This is one of a series of humorous books written by diverse authors and each blessed and approved by the nondeceased (yet) American comedy person Bob Odenkirk. Volumes in the OML include satire, cartoons, Black Humor, Gentle Humor, and Total Humor, and they cover a broad range of subject matter, united only in their tendency to provoke laughter and warm feelings of distraction. No textbooks or pornography will be included in the series (yet).

To Naomi. Thank you for indulging me.
Please continue to do so.

"Don't waste your money on that book—it's a lot of *hooey*."

—from Merriam-Webster's definition of "hooey"

CONTENTS

ONE SHOULD NEVER READ
A BOOK ON THE TOILET

*By Miss Sally Penberton, of Miss Sally's
Finishing School and College of Internal Medicine*

H ello!
　　Hello!

Now I am pausing for you to reply, "Hello, Miss Penberton, of Sally Penberton's Finishing School and College of Internal Medicine!" Very good, girls—except for you, Violet Madison. You sound like a cow. How many times do I have to tell you: one should never speak with one's mouth open! It is rude for a man to see your tongue before the wedding. Why buy the cow when you can see the tongue for free?

If you are reading this, you have opened and/or purchased Mr. Odenkirk's book, *A Load of Hooey*. I am delighted for you, as I'm sure it will guarantee a slew of laughs and between a galette cup and an oyster cup (approx.) of titters. Before you wade in too deeply, however, I would like to remind you all of the golden rule: One Should Never Read a Book on the Toilet.

There are as many reasons One Should Never Read a Book on the Toilet as there are appropriate forks to use at a pure-bred horse's wedding (thirty-seven). Posture may be the most important. There are appropriate postures for both reading and for defecating, and neither is compatible with the other. The ideal reading posture is brutally erect, in full dinner corsets (keep tightened to eight inches), one foot up on an ottoman made out of a deceased family dog's pelt, the book balanced on the tips of the pointer and ring fingers. No other fingertips may be involved. Three fingertips to read a book? HAHAHAHA GOOD JOKE, GIRLS!! I CAN'T STOP LAUGHING!

Conversely, the ideal defecating posture is the Rosebud. You pull your dinner or lounging corsets (whichever are made of the rarest whalebone) tighter and tighter until the feces are squeezed half inch by half inch out of your dainty anus (*daintus*). If you need to ask your mother or lady-in-waiting to help, feel free. Not everyone can get the Rosebud right every time! (P.S. I am still laughing about using three fingertips to read!! When would you ever need that many!!!)

Ideally, however, you shouldn't be on the toilet at *all*, let alone reading on it. Remember: there is no man to open the lid for you! Ladies should go through doors only if a man has opened them for her, and ladies should use a toilet only if a man has de-lidded it for her. For what is a toilet lid but a door for your asshole? I am not just an etiquette teacher and doctor, but a poet as well.

Properly utilizing a toilet requires certain steps that should not be changed. Do not arrive late to your toilet. Fold the toilet paper into an elaborate swan (lengthwise, then widthwise, make a tip, add real swan meat to taste). Attempt the Rosebud. Write a thank-you note to your butthole on the swan paper. Make sure to use proper penmanship—even if the note is to your butthole!

"Thank" your butthole by wiping it with the note. Flush, using only the pinkie, or the thumb, which is nature's pinkie.

Now, I am usually more than a little distrustful of sending My Girls to traditional physicians (i.e., people who have not graduated from my school of internal medicine). It is much more polite not to hang an indiscreet, impolite, "braggy" diploma on the wall, or, better yet, to have never graduated from medical school in the first place (itself the biggest brag of all). But don't be afraid to call your local physician if the Rosebud goes poorly. I have seen more than a few women who, while attempting to defecate with politeness, have "popped" (← science term??) an internal organ. I may not be a doctor, but I am an unlicensed doctor, and I can tell you that the Rosebud is worth it!

There are so many other places for you to read this book. YOU DO NOT NEED THE TOILET. That should be your mantra, along with "My dowry is not a toy." You could read this book in a townhouse that your husband bought for you! You could read this book on a yacht that your husband bought for you! You could read this book on the toilet!

O ho, did you catch that?! That was a test! You CANNOT read this book on the toilet! I am not just a poet, but a trickster as well.

Ho HO!

I don't want to scare you, but some very bad things have happened to women who do not respect the proper etiquette of toiletry and who Read This Book on the Toilet. Take, for instance, Miss Amanda Maple of New York. She was rumored to have bought this "haha-book," and could not wait to void herself before she began reading. She gave herself paper cuts on her *small treasure* to the extent that she could not bear children. Due to this fact, she was promptly *put down* behind her house by her husband. Was it worth it? Of course not. She didn't even get to the good part of the book (pp. 32–36).

Etiquette is a beautiful thing. It's what separates us from the animals. (The things that separate us from the animals, in order: etiquette, elaborate fences, long cigarettes, whalebone.)

So, ladies, remember all I have taught you. I wish you all the best of luck with both your reading and toiletry endeavors. Godspeed. Now I have to remove a kidney and replace it with a diamond.

BEGINNINGS, OR, A BEGINNING, OR, HOW THIS BOOK BEGINS

"Twas bryllyg, and ye slythy toves
Did gyre and gymble in ye wabe...
but this time, ye slythy toves weren't fuckin' around."
—from the trailer for *Jabberwocky 3D, the Movie* (2015)

How does one begin a book? A letter, a word, soon a sentence, then another, and suddenly, a paragraph is begotten—a two-sentence paragraph.

Dickens, Melville, Odenkirk, all have faced the same question, and only one has failed. Melville. "Call me Ishmael." Talk about giving up.

I was born in Berwyn, Illinois. At the time, the doctors declared, with deadpan gravitas, "Boy, six pounds, eight ounces." I was circumcised and remain so, unable or unwilling to grow a fresh foreskin in the years since. Unable, actually, as I have tried— I've used creams and pills and all manner of massage, but it's no use. Fresh foreskin forsakes me, it foils me, it fails to flower on the face of my glans. And that's the final bit of poetry in this book.* You're welcome.

---

* except for the poems

But enough about me. That's the problem with biographies, auto- or otherwise. They're all me, me, ME... How about other people? When I pick up a biography of President Harry S. (Sissilopolus*) Truman, I want to read about Winston Churchill! Immediately! All this "Truman did this, Truman did that"! Enough! I want variety! Give me choices, change the tune, throw some Harriet Tubman into my *Trump: The Biography*. It's not my fault—I have ADD; I got it from a toilet seat, the best place to write or read a book, despite what the finishing-school scolds tell us.

Anyway, I have, somehow, begun, and escaped Melville's curse...please read on.

---

* I think.

A PORTRAIT OF THE ARTIST

H e has never been interviewed. He refused to meet, do a phone interview, or sit still for this profile.

He has never made a film or painting, nor has he written a poem, taken a photograph, sculpted a bust, or "tried" to make "anything." And yet he has fascinated the art world and captivated New York society in the past year. He's been praised as "unfathomable at worst" and "bafflingly circumlocutory at best" by *Scene There, Done That* magazine. He scored a 12 out of 10 on *BaffleMags*'s "Scoring the Downtown Scene" and has been crowned a "Notable Nelly" in *ArtScrape Magazeen*'s middle-of-the-year wrap-up three times (in the same list).

When assigned to profile him by *BUTTLESCUT* magazine, all I knew was rumor and scuttlebutt. But investigating him only caused the rumors to solidify and the scuttlebutt to harden. All quotations below are from an info sheet distributed by his PR representative and are not in any way to be "construed as true."

He's a man of habits, believing they "simplify life and make room for brainstorms." As such, he wakes each morning at exactly 7:43 a.m., catnaps throughout the day, and goes to sleep at precisely three o'clock in the morning.

Every day he wears the same "uniform": moccasins, tuxedo pants, and a variety of pajama tops designed especially for him

gone missing!

by L.L. Bean. On his face he wears his signature duck-billed hockey mask.

He wears the same pair of underwear for a month, then puts a fresh pair over the old pair until he has twelve pairs on, at which point he knows New Year's is right around the corner.

Every day for lunch he eats two hot dogs sans buns, a slice of lemon pie, and half a bottle of Yoo-hoo drink, room temperature. He pours it all in a bowl, microwaves it, eats it like a porridge, and says it makes his mouth taste like "a food closet."

He puts a Christmas tree up once a week and decorates it, then takes it down the next morning and puts it on the street. He is hated by his garbage man.

He doesn't observe Tuesdays. He wears a watch he smashed on purpose at exactly 12:00. As a result, he famously missed his own birthday by three months.

He's had the same assistant for ten years—his cat, Rodolfo. He pays Rodolfo in crickets. His East Village apartment has been condemned for cricket infestation three times in six years.

He reads the Bible in Aramaic to himself through a bullhorn every night. "It's the perfect mix of the old and the new," he reports.

The artist has been baptized, circumcised, exorcised, and bathed in the Ganges—all within a hectic month of "self-discovery," though now he calls all religion "too literal to be believed."

He has three children by four women whom he has never met.

He adopted a man older than himself, whom he affectionately dubbed his "grandbrother" and with whom he trades birthday cards three times a year.

He claims to hate "all drawings."

He votes Republican, and claims to have loved Ronald Reagan "primarily for his silhouette."

His favorite TV show is *"Mayberry RFD* with the sound drowned out by a Grateful Dead live bootleg from Madison Square Garden 9/4/79…second half of the show only."

He throws a Super Bowl party every year the day after the Super Bowl and locks the doors once the prerecorded game "starts," unlocking them only when the game is over and the post-show recap has been capped. He invites only one person to the party: himself. He records himself receiving the invitation, sending in his RSVP, receiving the RSVP, greeting himself at the party, eating chips, and cheering on his chosen team. No one has ever seen these recordings and, according to him, "no one ever will—they're for me and my personal edification."

When asked to comment on his life and work, the artist's father, a retired plumber from Nyack, New York, simply shook his head and muttered, "That guy's a fraud."

The Bible, Dead Sea Scrolls Edition—Unabridged

"The Wolf also shall dwell with the lamb, and the leopard shall lie down with the kid; and the calf and the young lion and the fatling together; and a little child shall lead them, a blind child; a blind child who himself is lost. This child will have no sense of direction, and one leg shorter than the other—so the route shall be circuitous. The child shall have red hair and halitosis. The hair is insignificant; the halitosis less so. The child shall be dim of wit, incapable of complex thought, and unable to acknowledge contradictory truths or hold complex opinions. However, he shall have a kind face, for whatever that is worth. A kind face and an ability to compartmentalize— perhaps he will have some brain damage, that's not for me to say. But so it will be, for the last shall be first. They should turn the line around and face it the opposite way, for at the back end will be an intelligent, thoughtful, experienced, grown man; an expert at making progress. But that won't happen, for the expert will be despised. Anyway, everyone will die going in circles following an ignoramus. It will not be pretty."

"DIDN'T WORK FOR ME"

If you're ever feeling poorly about yourself, about your lack of achievement, your utter inconsequentiality, your ridiculous little life lived in the shadows—take a moment and write some Internet reviews of other people's work.

HUCKLEBERRY FINN

One Star — Didn't Work for Me
by *MisterEveryman*

First of all, I am a HUUUUGE fan of Twain. I've read every one of his books and loved them all, yet somehow I'd overlooked this one. Well, everyone in my "book club" at work told me I *"had to"* read this *"awesome" "classic."* So I splurged on a library card and gave it a go. SPOILER ALERT—it's TERRIBLE! A long river-ride to nowhere!! Literary masturbation at its most onanistic! What was Twain thinking? *He wasn't!* Huckleberry Finn, a nasty character, takes a freed slave down a river in a not-very-well-made raft. They see some things, almost tip over, blah-de-blah…the end. And it's all written in pitiful childspeak. Was Mr. Twain's keyboard broken? Sad. I returned it late and had to PAY a FINE! I ripped up my library card as well as the receipt for payment. I want my couple of hours back!

THE BEATLES' WHITE ALBUM

Zero Stars—Didn't Work for Me
by *MisterEveryman*

Let's be clear: I am a GINORMOUS *The Beatles* fan! I am! I have every one of their albums, including reissues AND their funny, funny Christmas messages to fans. I have over 60 bootlegs! But somehow, after all these years, the one album I'd never gotten around to was this infamous "unnamed" double set. When a temp at my workplace saw me wearing my *The Beatles!* tie and commented on it (she liked it), then found out I'd *never* heard the *"White"* album, she INSISTED I hear it immediately and ran down to get it from her car. I couldn't wait to plop it into the CD player, eager to hear more "The Beatles" brilliance. All I can say is: "I hate you Beatles, oh yes I dooo"! Spoiler Alert—It's TERRIBLE MUSIC! My ears almost jumped out of their sockets! I challenge anyone to find a melody—you can't! From the monotonous "Blackbird" to the *pointless Beach Boys ripoff* "Back in the USSR" to the *mean-spirited* "While My Guitar Gently Weeps" to the what-were-they-thinking-oh-no-they-weren't-thinking-they-were-riffing "Honey Pie," this album *aspires* to claptrap. No wonder they refused to put their faces on it!! Now I know why it has no title and is called "The White Album"—because you can't put the word "SHIT" on the cover of a record album. I tried to return it the next day, but the temp who lent it to me had prematurely quit, probably thankful she had finally stuck someone with this musical bogey!

FRANCIS FORD COPPOLA'S
THE GODFATHER ONE AND TWO

½ Star — Didn't Work for Me
by *MisterEveryman*

First of all I like and/or love ALL of Frank Coppolo's oeuvre: from JACK to SWORDFISH to GODFATHER 3—but somehow I'd overlooked these two. Everyone at work told me I had to see Francis Coppolo's "GodFather Number One and Two." Why? "Because!" they screamed at me, "It won some Oscars!" FOR WHAT?—TEDIUM?!! It's a mishmash rehash of stories that stumble and start and stop and then, suddenly, out of nowhere, there is a MONTAGE of VIOLENCE!! (BTW—*"montage"* is a French-derived word for "a filmmaker throwing up his hands and shouting, 'I dunno—YOU figure it out!'") And what was that baptism stuff about? Was that supposed to SIGNIFY something? Methinks someone's been hitting the ol' vino a bit too hard. GF #2 is MORE OF THE SAME…not good, kinda sloppy, point-less, and too "ethnic" for my taste—if I want a history lesson I'll go back to grade school! The only reason I give it half a star is because it spawned the excellent GODFATHER #3! See that one, miss this one, thank me, and *you're welcome!*

THE BIBLE, KING JAMES VERSION

Zero Stars
by *MISTER EVERYMAN*

First let me say, I am a massive fan of all of King James's writings. I love everything the guy wrote—and in the original language, too...OLDE ENGLISH!! But somehow, I'd missed this one. EVERYONE at my church said I "must" "absolutely" read this one—the "book of books," I think they called it. So I sat down and I read it. Every word. And all I got to say is..."meh." Uninspired sludge. As a book it makes a great doorstop! Nothing special. A lot of stuff about who is related to who and then some VERY QUESTIONABLE tall tales that, I guess, are supposed to make a point. The lead character of the second book has some magic powers, but I don't think Harry Potter has to worry too much about getting bumped off the hero shelf—the only magic power the Jesus character had for me was the power to conquer insomnia!! What a waste of every Sunday for a year!! Save your money, buy a large brass dog to hold your doors open for you. You'll thank me.

HER LAUGHTER

Before I married her, when Angelisse and I were first dating—furiously, ecstatically, hyperactively—the people of the town (New York City—look it up!) warned me that while my A'Lisse (short for Angelisse—I was always coming up with nicknames for her) was mesmerizing, enchanting, and overfull of sparkling qualities, she would also challenge me to my core with her single drawback. They told me this in whispered conversation, but also in a few e-mails, written in all caps.

I will share her solitary dark spot with you in time, but first let me attempt the impossible—to describe my Angel's positive qualities, a smorgasbord of human excellence.

Her mind was a diamond of endless facets, while also being a steel trap that spun on the edge of a pointed stick. I only wish I was mixing my metaphors and not simply describing her actual mind.

Her spirit—well, her spirit was simply un-put-downable. She searched out every chance of connection, refusing to walk past a single soul without grasping their essence with her eyes. As a result, we avoided crowds and summer fairs because it just took too damn long to get anywhere.

Physically, my Angel was a specimen nonpareil, with large eyes in shapes an almond would envy and thin, delicate wrists that a champagne flute would fucking despise. She had big boobs, as well.

And then there was her laugh. Her laugh surprised people, because when it came it came suddenly, and it made everyone hate her instantly. It wasn't a cackle. A cackle would have been fine. Everybody's heard a cackle, and you can usually get used to it. My thin-wristed Angie had a laugh that crushed hope. It made you want to drill your ears till they bled and then pluck your eyeballs out and step on them just for good measure. It destroyed all human goodwill and warm feelings, leaving behind a cold, smoking horizon of ash. The sound of her laughter left you feeling like you'd swallowed someone else's vomit, which ended up having pieces of glass in it…plus a tiny, swallowable atom bomb.

This, her laughter, was that single negative quality I mentioned earlier. Allow me to dig deeper into this massive black hole hidden within the very fabric of her twinkling firmaments.

Her laughter kept her from getting jobs! No matter how good she was doing in an interview, that laugh would come out and suddenly there was no vacancy. The one time she did restrain herself from laughing, she easily won a job at a neighborhood tchotchke and hardware shop. On her first day, her boss attempted to tell a simple knock-knock joke to ease her in to her new work-place. She laughed. Then he told her he was closing his business for a little while because he suddenly didn't feel so good. When she called to find out when he would reopen, she learned he had moved THAT VERY DAY and had sold the business to a scrap dealer. This was a family business we're talking about! He was the fifth-generation owner!

Her laughter dispersed entire crowds. Even crowds of people who'd paid for their seats! Once we went to a rock concert at one of those outdoor venues where you bring wine and cheese and lay out a picnic blanket, and they had a stand-up comedian open for the band. To everyone's dismay, she *loved* the comedian and his offbeat japes. By the middle of his act, the massive lawn was empty except for Angelisse and me! The crowd's wines and cheeses sat abandoned in little piles. People must have just said, "Fuck it, I'll buy more wine and cheese, I can't listen to another moment of that ear-raping laughter." Then, to top it off, the band refused to go on. They'd heard her laugh, too! And this was a jam band! They weren't even a good jam band—only two original members. The concert was a total wash. We didn't even get a refund.

Her laughter finally did us in as well. One time I saw a mother with a mohawk haircut pushing a baby carriage in Central Park and, without considering the consequences, I muttered, "Look out, Mommy's on the warpath." Angelisse laughed, the baby cried, two dogs jumped into the pond, a couple of boats capsized, and three horses went bonkers, tossing the policemen from their saddles. It was a nightmare scene that would have made Heironymus Bosch say, "You're fucking kidding me." At that moment, a part of me died—it was the exact part of me that had been tolerating her laughter all this time. So I turned to my "Gelisimahoney" and, with cold certainty, I declared, "Angel, my Angel...I have something to tell you, and I need you to listen to me and believe me. Will you do that?" Her willing expression told me she would.

"I can never marry you." This stopped her (and her laugh) in her tracks. An explanation was due, and not just any explanation—I needed the greatest explanation the world had ever seen. Inspired by her searching eyes and how much I hated her laughter, I went on.

"I can never marry you because I'm an illegal alien and I have AIDS and I am gay and I'm already married, twice, and I just took a job in another country as a…drug smuggler." Without letting all that sink in, I carried on, "I know this is a lot to process, but you must believe me. I am needed in Colombia to smuggle cocaine so I can care for my other wives and afford the daily 'cocktail' that keeps my immune system strong and, in addition to all of that, I just signed up for a two-year art installation placing black flags in the ice of the Antarctic in a circular pattern. You'll be able to see it from space."

She stared at me for a long moment, and then her laugh burst through again, bruising my soul and wilting the grass. I winced, everybody winced, and I said, "Also, I can't stand your stupid laugh. You gotta stop that. I mean it."

And so we went our separate ways. Now I'm lonely again, making dinner for one. But I still believe in love, and dream of meeting a taciturn woman with a sour air, few delights, and the inability to laugh at anything at all.

AN ANGEL OF THE LORD

An Angel of the Lord came unto me. I thought that was cool. Worth mentioning, anyways. It told me that I could ask any question I had and I'd get the truth. So I asked: "Which religion is right and true?" He thought for a moment and said, "I cannot specify by name, but TWO religions are true." "Two?" I said. "How can that be?" He shrugged and said, "What can I say... that's the way it is." I said, "Can you possibly help me narrow it down?" He nodded and said, "Okay, I shouldn't do this, but— I can tell you that Scientology is NOT one of the true ones. Does that help you?"

"No," I said. "No, that does not help."

Famous Quotations—Unabridged

———————————

"*If you can dream it, you can do it.* Not 'you.' I mean 'me.' I was talking to myself. Did you hear me just now? Forget I said that."

—Walt Disney

MY EDUCATION, OR,
THE EDUCATION OF A ME,
OR, I NOT DUMB

Everything I learned I learned on the streets. The streets taught me very little algebra and absolutely NO organic chemistry. Class was always in session, but there were no desks and no teachers responsible to check on attendance, so class may as well have never been in session. I'll tell you what, though, I learned that adults are full of baloney and kids are little shits, and I don't know how much more learnin' is really necessary.

At home I learned about love, and how to dole it out in tiny increments that never deplete the wellspring of self-involvement. When you give too much love too freely, you inevitably find yourself caught up in other people's messy lives. Yech.

My fashion sense came from sorting through old laundry and choosing the stuff on top.

Did I mention hip-hop saved my life? That's because it did not.

I owe my family for my sense of humor. I don't owe them money. I don't have any money. I've never been paid for anything.

Whew...did they leave yet? Good. Actually, I'm very very rich.

Famous Quotations—Unabridged

———————⯈•⯇———————

"*If you're going through hell, keep going.* But please stop screaming, it's not good for morale."
                                                    —Winston Churchill

LOUVRE AUDIO TOUR FOR
HOMEOWNERS

Welcome to the Louvre Audio Tour for Homeowners, English Language Version.

The Louvre is the world's most famous art museum and the most popular tourist site in Paris. With more than thirty-five thousand works of art and sixty thousand square meters of exhibition space, there is a lot to see. Choose any wing and start walking and this audio tour can begin.

With more than two hundred thousand visitors tramping through every year, the Louvre has wisely chosen hardwood floors over carpet. Carpeting would have meant vacuuming. Constantly vacuuming. I mean nonstop vacuuming. Trust me, these wood floors take their toll in blood, sweat, and waxing, so if you think we're getting off easy, think again. The notion of making people take off their shoes by the front door has been raised and dismissed numerous times. Can you imagine the disaster that would be? People taking the wrong pair of shoes, people forgetting their shoes and walking out into Paris with bare feet, people suing the museum because they got some disease from the gutters of Paris? Forget it, just forget it...not gonna happen.

When you get to the end of the gallery, turn right—or left, whichever way you want, it doesn't matter—and you'll see that most of the halls are lit by natural sunlight streaming through skylights. Nice, right? However, that doesn't mean this joint doesn't use up frickin' light bulbs by the case. How many frickin' light bulbs? More than 120 a week, and they're not easy to replace, either, my friend. Can you see how high some of these ceilings are? Those are some tall ladders we have to use. Heck, we've got guys who, all they do is change light bulbs. At least that's how it feels sometimes. Cripes. I'm not complaining, but whoever has the light-bulb concession across the street from this place is rollin' in it—it costs a pretty franc, I can assure you.

In fact, it takes a staff of more than two thousand to keep this place up, and that's not counting the security for all these paintings and statues and things. Have you seen the glass pyramid? I bet you'd hate to have to clean that! Trust me, you would, I've spoken to the people who have to clean it and they hate it. Guess how much Windex it takes to wash all of them windows? Tons. Two-point-two tons per year. We weighed it.

Speaking of security, what's to keep somebody from just walking over to a painting when things are slow and tearing it out of its frame, jamming it under their jacket, and wandering out the door, whistling all the way? Well, every single painting and statue is rigged with wires, and the slightest touch sets off an alarm. Plus there are more than two hundred cameras in the ceiling, all being watched over by guards in some room somewhere. Then you've got the guys who watch the guards and the guys who watch the guys who watch the guards. I'm joking, but it's not that funny when you get the bill at the end of the month. Sometimes we wish we had paintings that weren't so "special" or "rare," but try selling that idea at a board meeting, trust me—you get shouted down real quick.

Let's look at some of the paintings. What's the first thing you notice about the paintings in the Louvre? That's right: the frames are fancy. Some of them are nicer than the paintings! Guess what else they are? Dust magnets. It's crazy. It's like they generate dust! These things have to be dusted, gently, like every three weeks. You can't use Pledge on them, either, you have to use this super-gentle approved wood-oil concoction or they'll rot. I'm not making this up! It's a real pain in the ass. Still thinking of starting your own museum? You must be crackers.

Have you seen the paintings on the ceilings yet? Some of these rooms have as many paintings on the ceiling as they do on the walls! How did they get them up there? They have these giant scaffoldings and they have to put them together each time they check or clean or change a painting. The paintings are so far away you can hardly see 'em anyways. Plus, at least twice a year some French guy has to poke around up there with this long broom-handled duster or it would be cobweb city!

You may be wondering as you wander these halls, why did they have to make it so fancy? Let me tell you something, bub, people long ago, they had a lot of time on their hands. If I had lived five hundred years ago I wouldn't have spent my time carving a bunch of wood so it could be hung forty feet in the air somewhere, I would have been trying to invent air-conditioning.

Well, that's the basics of this place. After you see it, you have to admit, the Louvre is a heckuva museum—a real piece of work. If you find an open bench, grab it. Here's how many benches there are in the Louvre: not enough. I've suggested they put in a bench for every painting that's boring or just "eh," but no one listens to me or any of my "ideas" anymore. Whatever. You're probably pooped by now. Believe me, I know how you feel, I work here.

I think I'll play you some music now. Au revoir.

P.S. There's a Starbies in the lower level—see you down there.

PUTTING IT OUT THERE

If I were running for president, the first thing I would do is hold a press conference and get all my skeletons out of the closet and onto the table. A skeleton table, if such a thing exists—big enough for a couple skeletons.

B efore I announce my candidacy for president of the United States I want to comment on some rumors and accusations that I'm fairly certain will come to the fore as my campaign gains steam. I will warn you, I'm going to be more open than any candidate has ever been, so please usher the children out of the room now.

The first and foremost accusation will be that I have cheated on my beautiful wife, Betty.

I *have* cheated on my beautiful wife, Betty.

I have cheated on her more than once. More than twice. More than three times. I could go on like that, but you get the gist.

I have cheated on Betty in brief, one-night affairs, and a few long-term ones. I have cheated on her with men and women, and groups of men and women, and one person who was kind of an "either/or," if you know what I mean.

My beautiful wife, Betty, doesn't know about this, but we will be discussing it in private soon after this press conference ends, and then, later, in public, and finally, possibly, in a court of law.

Now, I have not always been a willing participant in these—
how shall I characterize them?—"sex games." Sometimes I was
drunk. One time I had a blindfold on. Twice I was paid. Once I did
it on a dare. But in at least thirty instances that I can recall I was
cooperative and willing, so don't get the idea that I'm a quick lay
or easy to blindfold. In fact, I put that blindfold on myself! The
media will, no doubt, suggest that there is something weird about
me wearing a blindfold while having sex with two people I'd only
met a few hours before, but I assure you that I was on Ecstasy and
I would have tried almost anything.

Now, a further word about my beloved wife, Betty. I have
been married to this same wonderful, understanding, occasion-
ally oblivious woman for thirty-two years. Through it all—all the
sex with other people, all the awesome nastiness—I have *stayed*
married to her, with a quiet pride in myself and what a good guy
I am. In all these years I have married only *one* other woman, and

darn these ol' books!

had but one second, secret family,
and this was in another state, more
than thirty miles away—and believe
me, the added responsibility, as well
as the commute, was no picnic.
My enemies will try to twist this
and accuse me of polygamy, but
it's not polygamy because neither
wife knew about the other wife and
I think polygamy usually means the
wives know about each other, right?
I'm not sure if I'm right about that,

but I'm sure I will find out soon after this press conference and I will get back to you with a definition clarified by a court of law.

So there you have it. I have committed adultery, pickpocketing, and general scumbaggery on a semiregular basis, and now you know. Did I fail to mention my pickpocketing? Well...I'm a pickpocket. I do it all the time. Can't help myself. I'm sure with the Secret Service around I'll be forced to cut back on that exciting little hobby. Then again, maybe they'll make it easier—it might provide cover for me...yeah, this is going to work great. Vote for me, and let the pocket picking begin!

Famous Quotations—Unabridged

—————⋙•⋘—————

"*Insanity is doing the same thing over and over again but expecting different results.* Also, if you see your friend's face mutate into all four members of the rock group the Beatles, that's a sign as well."

—Narcotics Anonymous Saying

MY MANIFESTO

I f you're reading this, then I am dead. If my plan has been carried out with any degree of success, then there are more than a few disgruntled people left in my wake, as well as a few disgruntled people AT my wake*—for reasons that will become obvious later in this document.

This is my Manifesto, the Rosetta Stone that will give meaning to my actions and sacrifice—so read it carefully. All CAPITALIZED words are meant to have greater significance than the other words that gather at their feet. Please read the CAPITALIZED words in a slightly louder voice inside your head to get the full effect.

I will now enumerate the ways in which I, and others, have been APPALLED, ANNOYED, and ASSAULTED by the WORLD in its current state of FESTERING ROT. Firstly, TECHNOLOGY has misled us, our INFRASTRUCTURE is crumbling due to neglect and malfeasance, CHEMISTRY is in a state of chaos and disequilibrium, and SOCIAL GRACES are practically nonexistent. These are just my bullet points—I have a lot to say, so wish me well, here are the SPECIFICS...

1. TECHNOLOGY must be DESTROYED or at least LOOKED UPON WITH SKEPTICISM. The TURNING POINT was the manufacture of the MOST RECENT iPHONE. Everything up

until then was PERFECT, and perfectly in line with Nature and God's wishes, but these new iPhones are just...well, I don't have the latest one yet, but...it seems TOO good, if you ask me. God is not blind, and he's VERY sensitive, and his wrath is manifest in many ways, not the least of which is THE WEATHER, which has been far TOO HOT lately—does that tell you anything? Think about it.

2 (or 1B). The INFRASTRUCTURE of our modern society is completely compromised due to overbuilding and LACK OF RESOURCES. The entire grid is compromised and cracking, its weakness showing everywhichawhere. There is a solid three-foot-in-diameter brick of pavement at the end of my street which is being pushed UPWARD, teetering, literally TEETERING on the PEPPER TREE ROOT that is growing violently upward underneath it. This is scraping the BOTTOMS of cars. Including MINE. Somebody FIX IT!

2B. CHEMISTRY has also failed and bewildered us as a people, and continues to baffle and bum me OUT. What is it? At what point have you broken things down enough and now you're just playing with increasingly SMALL PARTICLES that no one can see or even remember the name of? Everything smaller than "a teaspoon" is really not necessary and only serves to ANGER me and fuel my PLAN, which I will get to in a second.

3. Point three has been CUT. You WILL NEVER KNOW what point three was. I have NO PITY for you and am perfectly happy

to confuse the masses who seem to like terrible TV SHOWS as much as they like GOOD ONES. TV has gone down the crap-hole...and NO, that was NOT the third point.

4. MY BELT is too long. I had to add a hole to it and it looks homemade and crappy and the excess belt just hangs out there, FLAPPING ABOUT.

CONCLUSION: THE POLITICAL SYSTEM in America is the best in the world. Our Forefathers had FOREsight and we owe it all to them. But the ELECTORAL COLLEGE is the most outstanding aspect of this system. It keeps the IGNORANT masses from voting into office the latest YAMMERING IDIOT whose razzle-dazzle they fall for. PLEASE KEEP THE ELECTORAL COLLEGE. If the electoral college is STILL IN PLACE when I die, then you will know I completed at least one part of my PLAN as PLANNED.

MY PLAN

My plan is that I WILL participate in our unfair, unjust, technologically deficient, chemistry-burdened, politically superb society AS IT STANDS, without making WAVES. I will deviously and cleverly CARVE out a life of quiet acquiescence to the grave INJUSTICES that I have enumerated as this social order BENEFITS ME GREATLY as a WHITE AMERICAN MALE. How and ever, all the while I am living, I will WRITE DOWN MY IDEAS and keep them hidden from the world UNTIL MY shocking and preplanned DEATH from OLD AGE. This plan will call for steadfast patience and some degree of QUIET DESPERATION, but I am up for it! You have been WARNED!

I am sorry it had to end this way, but I needed to teach the world a lesson. I hope you enjoyed reading this interpretation of my travails and hero's journey, and that it has filled your memory of me with significance and purpose, and that you liked the capitalizations.

---

* UPON MY DEATH, at my wake, if you're going to have a small coffee-service area, somebody put a bowl of BRUSSELS SPROUTS out AS A SNACK...that'll show everyone.

I THINK I JUST MET GOD

It was down on the railroad trestle, over the river. I was minding my own business, taking a leisurely Monday-afternoon stroll.

This was, like, half an hour ago. Maybe forty-five minutes. It's about a twenty-minute walk, but I was waylaid.

Do you doubt me? I understand, but believe me when I tell you: I say it happened.

I was throwing rocks at other rocks in the water below, hoping to hear that magical "clunk" sound that rocks can sometimes make when they smack together. It was a contemplative, and at the same time violent, time waster.

I smelled something burning and I looked up and saw a bush with puffs of smoke arising over it. Not puffs, but a soft cloud. I thought the bush was on fire, but in a moment I heard a rustling, then a bright light pierced the sky above and a soft wind fluttered as though the universe had whiffled a fart right in my face—a gentle poot, pleasant of smell, a waffle of heaven's intestinal deliverance. Anyway, suddenly there appeared a being, alight with… well, light, afloating above the grabbled ground, for that area has a lot of rocks lying about, as well as some old tin cans once used as bait cans by unknown fishermen. Make of that metaphor what you will. "Fishermen."

He, and it was certainly a he—unless women grow beards

these days, and that may be the case but I won't speak to it here—
He (and I will capitalize that word when referring to this celestial
Presance—and I will also capitalize Presence AND misspell it
from here on out, out of respect and cantankerousness) beamed
his bright beams at me so I could barely see, but in time I made
out a wizened face aglow with warmth and welcome, yet the crin-
kles around his eyes foretold of a skeptical, slightly damning air.
The warm yet scolding gaze was what one would expect from the
true deity.

Astounded, I stammered, "Who are you? What...are you...
the pope?"

He laughed aloud, right in my face, at the notion. Here I was,
having been farted upon and laughed at all in the space of a few
seconds. I felt smaller than a raisin—a small raisin.

"Are you, then, something greater than the pope?"

To this He gave no answer but just shook his head in dismay,
as if to say, "Shut up about the pope, okay? Just don't bring it up
again. Thanks."

Now, our encounter lasted but a few seconds, and yet they
seemed like an eternity. Not a long eternity—not like He bored
me. More like a short eternity that was impressive and awe-filled—
the good qualities of an eternity.

In the course of our afternoon together, He had many things
to share with me. I don't expect it would be easy for you to believe
me, but I offer as proof a stone tablet that He wrote for me, right
there, using his blazing finger. On it He wrote a simple truth that
I took to mean all other truths were enwrapped within it. He
wrote: "Thou shalt proceed with grace and beneficence upon the

earth from here onwards, and thy people shall follow thee until the golden gates of tomorrow's tomorrow." At reading this, He could see my consternation, so He erased it! You heard me, He WROTE something into STONE, then He erased it from the stone. Like it was nothing. Like it was paper. But this was stone! MUCH harder to write on, and almost impossible to erase. Then He rewrote his command: "Get it together and we can do amazing things." This I understood, and I happily accepted the stone to bring as proof of my bona fides.

Small sidetrack: the stone never made it back. Halfway home I realized I was tired and my elbow was throbbing so I buried it. I cannot tell you where, because I did not mark it in case some thieves came along looking for stones that were written on that they could get and sell. But it's there. I don't mind if you look for it. You can look for as long as you want. That could be a good thing for you to do, actually, just keep looking. I'd appreciate it.

But be not saddened, for there was another proof forthcoming. A gold parchment upon which was written a directive to us. I held it in my hands and rubbed it with my fingers and sniffed it with my nose and I tell you it felt like parchment paper and smelled like parchment paper— kind of a machinelike smell, but very "parchmenty," if you know what I mean. Upon it was written, in bold serifed lettering: "Be Kind Unto Each Other." Now, I'm sure we'll be parsing that command for millennia to come, but to me it means to have a

unplugged, unhappy

thought for your fellow man, and not just friends or others who do you a solid. I believe He implied (by NOT being particular) that we should strive to be kind to ALL "others," including enemies and jerks. In fact, one could argue at great length and in a series of what I will call "epistles" that this statement can be shown to contain multitudes and it will demand multitudinous study and endless parsing. At least I hope so.

Where is this golden parchment? I forgot it where I was. My arms were full at the time, with the stone tablets and the golden plates.

Did I mention the golden plates? He gave me two of them as incontrovertible proof of his realness. Two the size of a ruler in length and half a ruler in width (twelve by six inches or so). Beautiful, shining, made of pure gold. On these were written nothing. He didn't want to deface them. However, when I asked if there was anything He would have written on them if He weren't so delicate of sensibility, He responded (not with words, but with telepathy): "Yes, I should like to fill them with rules of behavior and the proper dressing of food, as well as a laundry list of manners, and, finally, a few how-tos on killing one's enemies and burying the bodies in a crouching position. The list is long, really, and would surely fill both sides of these beautiful gold tablets, cluttering them, destroying their aesthetic impact entirely."

Where are the gold tablets, you ask? Unfortunately, they are lost to time. Yes, I know I've only been walking for forty-five minutes, but hey…time swallowed them up. I'm not sure where I was when I lost them to time, but it was somewhere between minutes thirty-two and forty-three, by my guesstimate. Please, do look for them. Look and look and look, but don't stop believing or you will surely NEVER find them! As they say, "You can't win if you don't play!"

So there you have it. I met God down by the trestle and now I am here to share the good news. I'm not saying everyone should follow me, or give me something called a "tithing" with which to do as I please, but it wouldn't hurt and I think it's what He would have wanted.

Famous Quotations—Unabridged

———————⟫◦⟪———————

"*If you tell the truth, you don't have to remember anything.* You can just be a big dummy who doesn't remember anything, ever, but who everybody trusts a lot. A big, stupid, dummy." —Mark Twain

POLITICIAN'S PROMISE

Hello, and let me begin by thanking the citizenry of this great state for electing me as your representative to the United States Senate. I've never been to Washington, so I haven't been tainted by its atmosphere or culture. Washington and its ways are a complete mystery to me, I assure you, so when I get there it won't be politics as usual. In fact, it won't be politics at all! Thank you for that standing ovation. Please, let me continue.

Since I know nothing at all about Washington, the first thing I'm going to do when I get there is buy a map. I want to get a sense of how the city is laid out. Are there any screwy roads that change their name and then back again, like you often find in big cities? I don't want to waste any time wandering around lost when I could be doing the people's work.

As a new senator I will need one big question answered right away: where do you eat? I want to taste everything Washington has to offer, from lobster j'toi to Chinese chop suey to hamburger à la greasy! And I won't skip dessert. From cakes to frozen yogurts, I want to try it all.

Next up, the sights and sounds. I want to feel the pulse of Washington. I'll see the bigger monuments and I'll search for the hidden treasures. I'll check out blogs and ask people on the street for recommendations. How about a weekend at the zoo? Do they

have a zoo? I'll find out. Maybe that will be on that map I'm planning on getting!

Once I have a working knowledge of Washington and the
greater Washington area, it will be time to get to work. But first,
how does Government work? What are these three branches I've
heard so much about? What color house does the leader of our
country live in? Where do the senators go, and what do they do
when they're not working?

Before my first term is up, I promise to take a guided tour of
the Senate. I'll meet real live senators and get to shake their hands.
How cool would that be? Imagine me, a senator, gaining entrée
into real senators' offices!

But before I "go Washington" on you all, I want you to know
I will take day trips. Historic Virginia, I'm right on your door-
step! New York and the delights of Broadway are just a train trip
away. Why stop there? Arizona is a short hop, skip, and a flight
to see some of what I've heard are the most colorful rocks ever
invented! By the time my term is over I may have to get a new
map...or two...or three.

I hope you're happy you elected me to Government. I know
I am.

[*A train whistle blows.*]

There's my train... I'm taking the scenic route—b-bye!!

HITLER DINNER PARTY
A PLAY

Do you have an amateur theatrical group? Get one! They're a big pain in the ass and not very rewarding, but you cannot perform the following playlet all by your lonesome.

At the core of dramatic mise-en-scène (spelling? meaning?) is the notion that there must be a crisis of some sort. I just made that up, but you can use it.

Presented here is a dinner scene, easily produced, that features bombs and flashes of fire offstage—also easy to bring to life and super-cool. More important, we have two curious couples doing a dance of sensibility and manners, quite modern in its way. Also, it's got Hitler.

SCENE ONE

SPOTLIGHT onstage opens on our guest couple, Fritz and Annette Schnitzelkrank. A Society Couple dressed for a night on the town, circa 1945, Germany. The couple speak to the audience, setting the scene.

FRITZ AND ANNETTE: Hello/Hi/Guten Abend/Good evening/ We are the Schnitzelkranks.

FRITZ: In the year 1942, my wife Annette and I were invited for a dinner party with Adolf Hitler.

ANNETTE: Over the years, we had many dinners with Herr Hitler and his beautiful Eva.

FRITZ: You see, I had the good fortune of rooming with Herr Hitler at art college. I had liked his work very much and I never hesitated to tell him so.

ANNETTE: When Adolf came to power, my dear Fritz was made top art professor at Berlin University!

FRITZ: Throughout the war we met the Hitlers at many social events. We never refused an invitation from *der Führer*! But as the war dragged on, our final dinner plans were postponed again and again until March of 1945. With the city surrounded and our brave troops running out of supplies and food, bombs dropping all around us—well, we found ourselves greeting darling Eva once more.

ANNETTE: Oh, she looked terrible! Before Hitler could enter the room she whispered one solemn request, which we, being two very excellent dinner guests, were determined to deliver on.

EVA BRAUN [*sotto voce*]: Oh, if you could do me a kindness—

FRITZ AND ANNETTE: Yes, of course! Whatever is asked, dear Eva!

EVA BRAUN: Whatever you do—

Hitler enters! Eva finishes her request sotto voce.

EVA BRAUN: —don't mention the war!

Fritz and Annette have no time to react as Hitler paces over to them.

He is somber and deeply distracted. Fritz and Annette muster smiles. Fritz begins a halfhearted Nazi salute, but Eva shakes her head "no!" and he quits it. Hitler hardly notices—

HITLER [*weary*]: Ah, Fritz and…uh…

FRITZ: Annette, my wife.

Hitler grunts. Eva steps in.

EVA BRAUN: Well, the night has finally come. It is a real pleasure to host you both again.

Handshakes and smiles all around until the screech of a bomb tears the moment in two. An awkward pause. Hitler breaks the tension:

HITLER: So, are we gonna eat, or what?

EVA BRAUN: Yes, Adolfy, we shall eat.

FRITZ: I'm so hungry!!

They cross to the table and gaze at their first course, a salad. Hitler breaks the silence, muttering.

HITLER: Salad.

Hitler starts eating; the others join in. Eva prompts her guests to say something.

ANNETTE: We were afraid we were late. So many streets are closed—well, they're impassable, due to—

She stops herself.

HITLER: Due to what?

FRITZ: Traffic. It's backed up. Buncha weekend warriors out there.

Hitler nods and smiles at Fritz.

HITLER: I wonder what I would have as a last meal. Did you ever wonder this, dear Fritz? What would your final meal be if you could choose it?

FRITZ [*Laughing nervously*]: Oh, I don't know. I...I would just eat...I wouldn't care.

HITLER: Surely you would care. If you knew you had, say, three to seven days before you would be executed, you had time to plan, and many resources at your disposal, what would you eat?

FRITZ: Well, I'm not much of a foodie myself. Annette?

ANNETTE: I don't eat dinner. Except socially.

HITLER: Last lunch, then.

ANNETTE: I don't know...salad. What we're eating right now.

Hitler stares at his salad, then pushes it away.

HITLER: No more for me.

Eva scowls at Fritz and Annette—wrong answers all around.

FRITZ: Well...well...

HITLER: Well, what?

FRITZ: Nothing. Just "well, well." I was reading the paper...
[*off Eva's scowl*] Sports section! Have you ever heard about the
Chicago Cubs baseball team in America? They're really having a
year, I'm told. At baseballing. [*No responses.*] Nobody?

Hitler is staring off into space.

EVA BRAUN: Perhaps our guests can tell us a bit about the small
matters of daily life at university. Small, delightful matters.

FRITZ: Oh, things are good. Nothing much going on. There's
the usual infighting. Not "infighting." Uh, what's the word. Tiffs.
People have tiffs.

HITLER: What kind of tiffs?

FRITZ: Nothing earth-shattering.

A BOMB whistles and crashes LOUDLY, shaking the furniture.

HITLER: What kind of tiffs?

FRITZ: "Tiffles." Not even as big as tiffs. "Where did I put my
hat?" "Are you wearing my hat?" "Haha, we mixed up our hats."
"We're such silly-billies!" That kind of thing. A lot of that.

HITLER: Must be nice.

Eva smiles at Fritz...good stuff. Fritz is energized—

FRITZ: Oh, it is, it is. It's wonderful! Low stakes! You should try it
sometime! I mean, join us at the university, someday. Do you ever
consider what you might do after...uh...later in your, uh, career?

Eva shakes her head, staring at her plate.

HITLER: You mean after the thousand-year Reich is up?

Fritz laughs.

EVA BRAUN: I think that's enough salad. Let's get the main course, shall we? [*She taps her glass to summon a waiter. No one comes.*] Where is that staff?

HITLER: They're in the bunker. They can't hear you.

Hitler grabs Eva's fork to stop the tapping. A bomb explodes outside.

HITLER: I'm sorry. This is my fault. I do apologize. I think I've made a mistake.

ANNETTE: I hope you don't mean that you made a mistake in having us to dinner. We do so love to dine with you and darling Eva—

HITLER: I was talking about the war. World War II.

ANNETTE: Yes…I'm familiar with it.

FRITZ: Oh, Herr Hitler, I wouldn't call it a mistake. I think you're being a little hard on yourself—

HITLER: What would you call it then? A boner? Did I pull a "real boner"?

Eva tries to stop him—Hitler waves her off, turning to Fritz, raging—

HITLER [cont'd]: Tell me, old friend! Say it to my face! Tell me

I pulled a boner! Somebody, say it!

FRITZ [*meekly*]: You pulled a boner.

HITLER: There! Finally. Someone said it. What a fucking relief! Jesus H. Christ. That took long enough.

FRITZ: I...still like your artwork.

HITLER: Well, you're an idiot.

Lights fade as the sound of bombs rises.

Famous Quotations—Unabridged

———————⟫-◦-⟪———————

"*Don't walk behind me; I may not lead. Don't walk in front of me; I may not follow. Just walk beside me and be my friend.* Or we could skip the walk and just be pen pals. Let's do that instead. It's cold out."

—Albert Camus

MY SPEECH TO THE GRADUATES
OF THIS FINE INSTITUTION

Hello, young people. Today is a momentous day. Today you are stripping from yourselves the protective husk of "student" and stepping into the harsh, naked, unforgiving fluorescent light of adulthood. I don't envy you, unless you have a massive penis. If you have a massive penis, this speech is not for you. You can just daydream for the next few minutes. Think about the women you will soon be having sex with in a series of porn films. Do me a favor: can you not look into the camera when you appear in those porn films? In fact, tell the director not to allow the camera to ever show your face. I don't want to see it. Seeing men's faces in porn immediately kills my "zest," if you will. Thanks, sorry about the sidetrack, but it's important to seize the moment when you have the attention of a potential celebrity.

To the rest of you, who won't be appearing in porn films— well, maybe some of the women will go into porn, and to you I say: good job, thank you, and I'm sorry—all three at once.

To those who remain, here is my only advice: finish college, don't take advice from strangers, and enjoy all the porn you "accidentally" see.

G'night Cleveland!

Famous Quotations—Unabridged

———————⇒►◦◄⇐———————

"*If I have seen further it is by standing on the shoulders of giants.* When I have failed miserably, that, too, was on the shoulders of giants—giant fuckups, that is." —Sir Isaac Newton

WHAT I'M LOOKING FOR
IN ANOTHER MAN

A ll right, ladies, back off! You're not the only ones looking for a good man in your life. I may be a man myself, but that doesn't mean I am all I need. I want a companion—more than that, I need a helpmate, a bro, someone of the "rougher sex" to applaud me and be by my side as I navigate the vagaries of this life. I'm prepared to describe this hunk to save myself from having to suffer through a bunch of interview/back-rub sessions, so back off and butt out. Speaking of butts—

First of all, I'm not looking for a "hot bod" or a cute butt. Frankly, I wouldn't know a cute butt if it bit me in the ass. My dream dude must have a sense of style so he can help me pick out clothes that fit together instead of me just grabbing the first thing on the top of the pile. I'm forty-eight years old and my clothes are still kept in a "pile," so I need this guy, pronto. He will probably be gay, because none of my straight friends are any good in this department. So gay is fine—but again, no cute butt necessary. A cute butt would just be wasted on me.

He should have wonderful, piercing, clear eyes. By that, I mean his eyes must be clear for him to see out of, and his clarity of vision should pierce through smog and low-lying fog. My eyes aren't doing so well: things are getting watery and I've always been color-blind. My guy mustn't be color-blind! I need him to tell me what's in front of me, especially when we're out racing in his car.

He should have a car, and oh! What a car! A stylish mini-convertible like the kind James Bond would drive. We could take it for spins in wine country—even with the low-lying fog (see above), and I could drive superfast around those hairpin turns because he would be using his piercing eyes to see oncoming danger, and we'd never, no, never, get lost (see below).

Mr. Hotstuff must have a good sense of direction so he can orient me to where my GPS is trying to tell me to go, because sometimes GPS stands for "Getting Places Circuitously," if you know what I mean. This magic dude could even reroute me entirely if he felt like it. By "reroute" I'm not trying to be metaphorical—again, I'm not gay, and I'm not planning to "turn" gay.

You know what? Now I'm thinking my "perfect fella" should probably be homosexual. The position shouldn't even be open to anyone else. I need diversity. I need to open things up. Heck, I'd like him to be one of those guys who knows what women are thinking. He can help me interpret cryptic signals from my wife, like when she tells me she's "had it" with me. What does that mean? Is it a come-on? If so, it's not very sexy.

He doesn't need to be a hunk, but he should have upper-body strength like a mule, because guess what? We're going to be moving some furniture! More specifically—can my hottie's fore-arms be sinewy and scrawny like a pterodactyl's? So he can reach through gratings for dropped keys, and under cracked windows to turn levers to lift the window so I can crawl through and unlock the front door when I lock myself out? Better yet, just make him a certified locksmith!

Let him be well-read, so he can tell me what happens in *The Great Gatsby*—that thing always tires me out before the end. Also, may he have a rhyming dictionary in his head for when we're in the car making up lyrics and laughing. He doesn't have to be good at Scrabble, though…it's okay if he puts up a fight, but I want to be winning, mostly.

I don't know if the guy I'm dreaming of is out there. Then again, maybe there are quite a few gentlemen who would work for me—I'm just starting this process. If I meet more than one outstanding man, then it'll come down to a personality match— or maybe I'll just be forced to pick the guy with the cuter butt.

Famous Quotations—Unabridged

———→•←———

"*You must be the change you wish to see in the world.* If you want things to be more fun, bring toys and Frisbees with you. If you want things to be more attractive, dress up a little. If you want things to be warmer and brighter, light yourself on fire, or something. What do I care what you do? Now, are you gonna finish that?"

—Gandhi

THE PHIL SPECTOR I KNEW

I n a decade of friendship, Phil Spector, Mr. Wall of Sound, has gone from being an acquaintance to a friend to, finally, my BFF of all time. Phil's a wonderful, talented, sweet man, and in a decade of laughs, life, and life-ter (laughter and life), he has enriched my world with music, good conversation, and gunshots. This is my story of him, and, if you must know, us.

HOW I MET MR. WALL-OF-SOUND

Fifteen years ago, I was working at the Fatburger on Santa Monica Boulevard, seating people (not an official position, as they reminded me every five minutes), when his Phil-ness came in with bodyguards at three a.m. to get a chili-egg-pizza burger. I immediately put some of his songs on the juke and won him over with my grins and head-bops in his direction. He could tell I was a fan, and what's more, that I was unencumbered by employment or responsibility, and so he invited me back to his "castle" at Alta Loma. I got in that limo and never looked back. (I was facing the back of the limo, so I would have been looking forward if I looked "back.")

That first night was a party that has (metaphorically) continued to this day (it's Tuesday as I write this). Sir Phil took me home. There were a couple of nasty hookers whose names shall remain unremembered, and the party started Spector-style when Phil playfully brandished a gun, playfully herded us into a listening room, and playfully wouldn't let us leave until we heard his Christmas album ten times in a row.

Since that time there have been many actual (non-metaphorical) parties, too many to recount. But they have all had that same exciting mix of "hail fellow well met" and "I'm gonna shoot you if you don't do what I tell you" energy, blended just so, everything "pushed to its limit": an experience I have come to call the WALL OF FUN.

Let me testify to his character. Phil has only shot me three times in ten years. Granted, he has shot AT me around fifteen times, and granted he has shot at the walls and ceiling near me approximately thirty-seven times, but when you take into account how many times he has shot a gun off around me, or, more important, how often he has merely *brandished* a gun in my presence (125 times), then being shot three times is not very much. Keep in mind—we were *partying*. This was a GOOD time.

Now, if you'll get off your high horse for a moment, I will let you in on something else. Of the three times that Phil has shot me,

dreaming of his beep-boop

he has only killed me TWICE, and of the only two times he has killed me, he has only shot me in the face ONCE, and, sorry to step on your sick fantasies—he has never had sex with my corpse. It goes without saying that as I am writing this, I have been revived— brought back from the dead—every single time Phil Spector has killed me. Uh-oh, did I rain on your parade? Boo-hoo. I'm so sorry.

I'll tell you some more secrets that may ruin your simplistic assumptions. Phil only shoots near you or at you if you're *already* a friend. That's right. You're not a true pal until you've been "tapped." It's an honor. See, he lives by a code. He never shoots in anger, only in fun: when he's partying, or working, or when you're in the same room with him.

WAS IT ALL WORTH IT?

Phil's talent and contributions to American music far outweigh his murderous and threatening behavior. One thing that's often been overlooked is how important the "wall of sound" is to American music. The wall of sound has generated some of the greatest records of the last forty years. These are songs that play on the radio constantly, and especially in nostalgia-themed diners. It's an inspired sound, and listening to those records often makes you nod your head in brief recognition before you go back to eating your burger and worrying if your car is being ticketed. What a gift he's given us!

The point is, my Hollywood friend is no longer free to roam and party and shoot at me, so you'll have to excuse me if I seem kind of down. I'm not. I just don't feel as jumpy as I did when my pal was around. Miss ya, Phil, thanks for (mostly) missin' me.

Kisses.

Gunshots.

Famous Quotations—Unabridged

When asked by an associate "How long should a man's legs be?" Abraham Lincoln thoughtfully responded, *"Long enough to reach the ground!"* Then, after another think, he added, "They have to make it up high enough to reach his torso, as well. Basically, they must go from the base of the stomach to the shoes...and the feet should fill the shoes completely. Did I mention the knees? One for each leg should do the trick. Yes, that's good enough for me— frankly, I'm more interested in his ass—" And at this the great lawyer was cut off.

MEANINGFUL POEM

IF I HAD MY LIFE TO LIVE OVER AGAIN

If I had my life to live over, I'd dare to make more mistakes.
I'd risk more, go out on a limb. I'd take longer walks, feed the
    ducks in the park.
I'd wear thicker socks, and eat more ice cream.
More ice cream—and a better brand of ice cream.
With a *higher fat count*.
Gourmet ice cream.
In fact, I would stick mostly to gelatos.
I would notice every bird and give it a name,
and write that name in a tiny notebook.

But let me return to the issue of ice cream.
I wouldn't confine myself
to national brands.
I would travel the countryside eating the regional equivalent of
    premium ice creams.
And if I were eating ice cream with you, I would steal yours
    when you looked away.
If you never looked away, I would badger you through the entire
    feast—

"Are you going to finish that? Are you done? I'll finish it if you
    don't."
Until you gave in.
For, you see, I have been one of those people who eats an entire
    box of "lite" ice cream
with fewer calories!
Who orders three scoops of ice cream and says, "Make one of
    them sorbet!"
Who offers to *share* the "death by chocolate" dessert.
I have even eaten an entire box of "dietetic" ice cream
    sandwiches
in one sitting.

What was I thinking? I should have just eaten the regular kind
    of ice cream sandwiches. I have even eaten popsicles when
    there was a Häagen-Dazs retail outlet nearby.
I did that twice.
Believe me, I remember.
But if I had to do it all over again,
I would eat even more.
And I can't restate this enough:
A higher fat count.

In fact, forget that stuff I said at the top about walking in the park
and the bird-naming dealy.
If I had my life to live over again, I would focus on the getting
    and eating of ice cream.

MARTIN LUTHER KING JR.'S
WORST SPEECH EVER

I n the midst of the Freedom Riders summer, King was called upon to give a speech at the Rock of Abernathy Baptist Church in Abernathy, Mississippi. It was a hot summer, even for Mississippi, and King had had weeks to prepare this speech, but for some reason he dillydallied. If he was betting on rising to the occasion, he lost that bet.

People in attendance that day remember the speech as "the opposite of a shining moment" and "terrible." Abernathy's Reverend Fulton Slocum dismissed it as "a total waste of everyone's time."

While there is no medical proof, King scholars have ascribed his complete oratorical failure to "possibly low blood sugar" or "simply the greatest brain fart ever."

Here, then, is a transcript of Martin Luther King Jr.'s worst speech ever.

LOOK UPON THINE FLYING EYEBALLS
by M.L.K. JR.
As transcribed, verbatim, from the actual event.

Uhh. Um. Hello. Hi. I was not told I would be speaking today, but, I guess—I'm Martin Luther King, I'm invited to a church, should've put two and two together.

[*To himself*] You can do this, King, come on, get it together.

[*To the crowd*] We stand together today, all of us, black and .
white. Well, there's not so many white people here. [*Squinting*]
Maybe some in the back. Not important, moving on.

All of us here today are a great conflagration! What? That's
not the word. Congregation. Not the same thing.

[*Wipes his brow*] Whew—it is hot in here. Man, it's hot here in
the great state of Kentucky.

[*Whispers to the side*] What's that? Alabama? Mississippi?
Okay, Mississippi. So why did *that guy* say Alabama? Yes, you
did. You guys heard him. Whatever. That's what I get for asking
the peanut gallery to opine.

[*To himself*] Let it go, Martin. Back on track—

We stand together. Some of you are sitting, I know. But in your
hearts you are standing! You are standing! No, you don't have to
stand up. Sit back down, please. Don't listen to me. I mean, listen
to me, but don't do what I tell you to do. Just sit back down.

See, I can see into your hearts—your happy, hopeful hearts,
some of them hurting, all hoping to heal. What the heck's with the
letter *h* all of a sudden?

[*To himself*] Back up, King, get on track here.

Your hearts can see—they do, they can see better things. The
eyes in your hearts are hopeful! Hopeful eyes that fly with wings!
Blind to hatred, blind to retribution. Blind eyes that fly! Think
about that! Boy oh boy oh boy, that's something, isn't it? That…
strains credulity.

Let me begin anew. Let us all begin anew: me with the talking,
you with the listening.

Can I get an "Amen"?? I can't? Okay…par for the course. Wrap it up, Martin.

Okay…what I'm thinking of is…a metaphor. A glorious metaphor like a shining beacon. A profound, top-notch metaphor. Imagine, for me, if you will, a metaphor for suffering, for sorrow, for persecution, but also for redemption, for joy, for celebration. Wouldn't that be great? Wouldn't it? Is this mic on?

Okay, that's all I got. I still have time? How about I do a Q and A? No? No questions? Criminy, it's a steam bath in here.

Famous Quotations—Unabridged

———✺◦✺———

"*Two things are infinite: the universe and human stupidity; and I'm not sure about the universe.* But that might just be me being stupid."

—Albert Einstein

FREE SPEECH FOR ALL!

*Below is a FREE speech that you can use for ALMOST ANY EVENT.
Please give me credit for it if anyone asks, but I'm not going to charge
you anything…it's on me!*

Just STEP UP TO THE MIC AND BEGIN:

W ell, they said it couldn't be done. But look, just look at all of you! Heroes. A roomful of heroes. You're all astronauts, right? I was told I would be speaking to a roomful of astronauts today. Okay, that's fine, I'll still talk to you people. You look enough like astronauts. My main point is this: they said it couldn't be done! They did. But look at all of us, right here, right now. It's being done.

That's not all they said, though. They also said, "Why try?" And: "Don't bother!" Also: "There's no point!" They called it "a waste of energy, time, and planning!" Naysayers! One person even said, "Nay"! What's his deal? Does he think this is the Middle Ages? Forget that guy!

Oh, but they said other things as well. One guy said, "I think it can be done but I won't help. I'm too busy—I've got to pick up laundry and yadda yadda yadda." I didn't hear the last part of what he said—I had headphones on. The point is, that guy is NOT HERE right now. Screw him.

One lady said, "I think it can be done, but I don't want to clean up afterwards!" That lady IS here today...ma'am, will you stand up? Where is she? I can't see her. You cowardly witch! Lady, you don't have to clean up because we'll *all* clean up! Right, everyone? No...Okay, I got a better idea, let's just not make a mess, then NO ONE has to clean up. Sound good? Good. Now shaddup, lady!

Now, let me address the guy who brazenly told me that he knew it could be done because—and this took some real cojones—because he'd *already done it*! No. I don't think so, pal. I don't think you already did it, because then it would be done and what would be the point? There would be no point. But there is a point and it is this: It can be done. We can do it. We're doing it.

But I'll go one step further. I think it can be done in *record time*. Today. Starting...now! So thank you for being here, thank you for believing, screw the naysayers, and LET'S GET THIS OVER WITH!

A HAZY CHRISTMAS MEMORY

Sweet Christmas!

As I entered Momma's kitchen I smelled the sharp whiff of crushed pine needles swaddled in strains of cinnamon, the aroma of baking cookies—cinnamon cookies!

Wait, no, hold the phone, there were no cookies. We couldn't afford cookies that year.

But there were almonds! Yes, I recall a whiff of almond, as aperitifs were distributed amongst the becalmed adults.

Scratch that—it was BEER! Almond-scented beer. That's why we couldn't afford the cookies—we needed to buy the Christmas beers!

On third thought, there *was* no almond scent! The beer smelled like beer. In fact, the beer smelled like *old* beer. The adults were drinking (and spilling) beer! That's what I smelled—I'm almost sure of it!

Maybe someone was eating almonds. That must be what it was—almonds and beer. No, wait, nuts and beer. Or a nut mix—that had almonds in it. Yes, I can stand by that—beer and beer nuts were the smells that wafted about my excited nasal receptors.

Blessed Christmas!

We didn't have a real tree—so nix that pine smell. PINE-SOL! Yes, that's what it was, the dagger-sharp scent of Pine-Sol emanating from the bathroom. This was on a Wednesday…or possibly Thursday. It was definitely one of the days of the week, that I can say with some degree of certainty, and Christmas was nearby, or in the recent past.

Oh, Christmas.

I'll be honest, I don't remember stuff very well. Except for regrets. I've got a photographic memory for regrets, which it turns out is unnecessary and burdensome. Still, for your amusement, I will keep digging…

The sounds of Christmas! Such sounds!

A cacophony of voices! Seven children jostling and fumbling through a mound of winter clothes, shouting plans for a busy snow day. "That's my glove!" "That's my boot!" "Give me some room, I'm try'n to get dressed here!" "Somebody just kicked me in the teeth!" A police siren, somewhere in the distance. Or possibly in the driveway—my godfather was a cop who liked to drink and "play" his siren.

But oh, it was cold out! Bitter! Or maybe not so bad. It might have been warm. Let's go with "lukewarm." It was a fine, Christmastime lukewarm outside, so us kids didn't spend too much time getting dressed, and there wasn't any snow. I know for a fact that we did fight a lot. Or maybe we didn't. Maybe we weren't fighting at all—maybe we were caroling. Yes, that's what it was, the sounds of children caroling. Sounded like a bag of cats.

The family, always the family, at Christmas!

Each of us took on a special task. I was assigned to spend the day with my aunt Frank on a search for a Christmas staple—mint chocolate candies to be frozen to a cold crisp.

My aunt Frank, who smelled of tea and cement, wore saggy jeans and a tattered Chicago Bears knit cap with the logo half-fallen off. She was either a man or a lady of such wizened age that one didn't publicly comment on

finders, beepers!

her sex. She lived alone, or with another old man-woman, down-town, in a neighborhood that had once been ethnic but was slowly becoming…less ethnic.

As Aunt Frank and I traversed the town we would munch on warm egg-salad sandwiches. She would chew and chew and describe her latest visit to the doctor and I would watch her jaws roil, frothing with bits of white and yellow and pickle. Damn you for making me remember this! Anyway, I think she was a man in the end.

Off we would go on our appointed rounds. We would drive around town in circles, searching for these waxy chocolates that had somehow, by accident perhaps, become a custom in our house (along with the beer-drinking I mentioned). Eventually we would find the damn things and bring them home to a gentle chorus of baffled burps.

Holy Christmas!

And if I'm not mistaken, there was a story told each year, a fairy tale about someone named "Jeebus." I'm getting his name wrong, I'm sure. Josey. Jesus. Jesus H. Chriminy! That's it. What a strange name. He lived long ago, and he spent his life trying to find the brightest star in the sky. He made the first zombie! And though he was a man full of joy and love, at the same time, this man—whom I never met—was deeply disappointed in me on a very personal level. Yes, this *Jesau* fella had something against me. Which makes no sense, I know, so I can't be remembering it right.

Anyway, Christmas…was that really what we called it? Bottom line: there was a lot of disco music, a tree got knocked over, and there was a naked man dancing barefoot in the snow. That's all I'm sure of right now.

oh my, no- I'm in fine fettle! In fact, my doctor says I have the body of a 65-year-old GAY MAN!
We get it. You're very old and very gay.
Yes, but do you support me, Burt? I can see this is hard for all of you- They say "it gets better," and I surely hope that it does.

Is that it, Dad? Is there anything else?
I'm glad you asked, Gibby. I want you to meet someone...

Rod and I are together now.  We're not monogamous...yet, but I have high hopes. So, you see my delectable story has a happy ending after all, don't you agree?

Hmm — well, if you won't agree I'm sure Rod will. What do you say, lover? Are you going to give me a happy ending?

You got it, Sweet cheeks.

fin

Famous Quotations—Unabridged

"*Don't cry because it's over. Smile because it happened.* You won the frickin' lottery, man. You're rich! It wasn't even that fun to 'play'—all you did was buy a stupid ticket!"

—Dr. Seuss (Theodor Geisel)

BASEBALL PLAYERS' POEMS ABOUT SPORTSWRITERS AND SPORTSWRITING

"ELEGIAC"

What does the word
"elegiac" mean?
What about "pastoral"?
And "contemplative"?
Why do you
Keep calling
Baseball all these weird French names?
Stop it.
Douchebag.

THE BLANK PAGE

Fat fingers dance across
the clattering keyboard
Grinding out meaning
Ennobling the actions
Of real men doing something tangible
for a living
And not sitting on their asses
"analyzing" shit.
Pathetic.

SPRING TRAINING

A gin and tonic for breakfast,
plenty of sunscreen,
a note pad.
A hot dog.
Fat ass
Planted in the stands.
Taking it all in,
gorging yourself.

SPRING TRAINING pt. II

Later, alone
in a motel room,
farting.

INSTANT ANALYSIS

We played hard
We lost
End of story.
You, however,
are the real loser.

Famous Quotations—Unabridged

———◆◇◆———

"*The Buck stops here.* Seriously, I will not give you even one buck, this one stays right here, in my hand. I don't care if you're a girl scout and I already ate half the cookies, I'm the president, I can eat any cookies I want and I DO NOT PAY." —Harry S. Truman

THE ORIGIN OF "BLACKBIRD"

P aul McCartney was generally seen as the generous, "upbeat" Beatle. However, some claim he had a well-hidden dark side: envious, resentful, belittling. If that's true, it rarely showed. Evidence of this tendency in McCartney can be found in abundance on the day he premiered the song "Blackbird" to the other three Beatles. Unarguably a masterpiece, it was also written and arranged by McCartney alone. Legend has it that "Blackbird" came to "Macca" fairly easily and completely, with almost no conscious effort on his part. Despite being a solo creation, "Blackbird," like all Beatles songs, is attributed to "Lennon/McCartney." This shared-credit situation has been known to irk McCartney, and yet even that tension doesn't explain the unbridled assault of sarcasm and peeve that issued from "the cute Beatle" on this singular occasion.

August 18, 1968, Abbey Road Studios, Studio 4, 11:15 a.m. Engineer's notes:

Band members came in fairly early (and fairly shagged-out) from another night of "creams and ales and whatnot." Mini jam session. Lennon kept asking Starkey to "play quieter" and finally to "Stop! The drums in me head are all I need." After a tea-and-jam-butties break,

McCartley [sic] grabbed an acoustic and said, "Here's something, see what you think," then played a song called "Blackbird" in its entirety. Excellent song. Excellent, excellent song. Unbelievable song. Like God humming. When he finished, he suddenly became vituperative...

Transcript from the audio tape:

McCARTNEY [*As the final notes of "Blackbird" ring out*]: Well? What do you think? Anything to it? "Ugh," right? Don't say anything! I know. I'm sorry. Get the trash bin out! I'll reimburse for the studio time. Please forgive me...

RINGO: Well, I thought it was really pretty...

McCARTNEY: Stop—it's no "Octopus's Garden"! Am I right? Let me play it again, in its entirety, just the way it came to me, when I was alone, writing it...

[*McCartney plays "Blackbird" again, from beginning to end, and again, it's an impossibly beautiful and perfect composition. The other Beatles stare at their shoes.*]

McCARTNEY: Garbage, right? Yeesh! I am so sorry. SOOOOOO sorry. George, please forgive me. Do favor us with another of your sitar explorations so as to wash the taste of that dreck from our ears! Do, please! Where's the sitar? Hurry, get a sitar!

HARRISON: Well, I liked it...

McCARTNEY: Shows what you know! I'm sorry. I'm just embarrassed. John! The Great John Lennon! Sir, I am so sorry to waste YOUR time with that!

LENNON: Well…it's a little lullaby-ish for my taste, though.

McCARTNEY: Of course! It's just a throwaway lullaby! People hate lullabys! They're awful, awful! John, save the day and yowl us all one of your patented free-form political diatribes to obliterate the memory of my gummy treacle!

HARRISON: Look, man, I think your sarcasm is unnecessary, you know? It's going to be on the album and all, there's no need—

McCARTNEY: Oh! Do you think it'll make the album?? Oh, will it?! Oh, thank you, George! Thank you! You deign to have one of my songs grace the next Beatles album? Because usually I do have to fight pretty hard to get my usual 90 percent of the songs on there next to your 10 percent! Oh, joy! Did you hear that, Ringo! I'm going to have a song on a real Beatles album! Me, Paul McCartney!

[*At this point, Harrison rises to leave—*]

McCARTNEY: Don't leave! Don't leave, please, we need you to noodle around in the background! Where's that sitar?

[*Harrison slams the door—*]

McCARTNEY: Oh, no! Now who will noodle around? Nobody?

LENNON: Look, man, we get it, you wrote a perfect song. Congratulations, but really, I mean, what's next?

YOKO: [*unintelligible "artistic" clucking noises*]

McCARTNEY: YOKO! Is Yoko here? There you are, dear, under the covers! Do you play the "bed" now? Is it an instrument?

Uh-oh, have I accidentally given you a new idea for a performance? Oh well, by all means please scream out one of your bloodcurdling antisongs to strip away the execrable beauty I just plastered all over the room because I just wrote the greatest FUCKING MELODY EVER FUCKING FUCK-WRITTEN! Let's hear it one more time just to check—

[*Paul plays "Blackbird" again...and again, it is a perfect song. Note: no overdubs needed.*]

McCARTNEY: Yup: THE GREATEST SONG EVER WRITTEN! Glad I double-checked! Hey, where's everybody going?

[*The remaining Beatles have left the room. McCartney, exhausted, stays behind and plays "Blackbird" to himself three more times, smiling the entire time.*]

I MISSPOKE

I'm Rod Blogbert, candidate for Senate, and I approve this message.

Rape is an awful act. The other day, in a TV interview, I misspoke. I used the wrong words—*guilty,* and *pleasure*—in the wrong way, and for those words, in the order they came out of my mouth, I apologize. The letters in the words were also at fault for having lined up in such a manner so as to form those wrong words, but since I am going to need those letters to deliver this apology, I'll go easy on them—this time.

As a candidate running for Senate, I want justice: both for the victims of sexual assault and for myself, for misspeaking. We have both been wronged.

I have a compassionate heart, and right now it hurts—for those victims, as well as for my political career. The mistake I made was in the *words* my mouth spoke, not in the heart I have. If my heart had its own mouth, it would never have spoken those words in that order.

But, I am sad to say, my mouth is not alone in its dastardly malfeasance. My lips formed many of the consonants I used in my interview, but they could not have done so without the cooperation of my teeth and tongue. Together, this "troublesome trio" conspired to misrepresent the intentions in my heart by forcing my mouth to emit sounds that in turn suggested that rape victims may experience something other than a horrible violation. I'm not certain how much my lungs had to do with all of this. I suspect that neither lung was aware of the scandalous, offensive, utterly retarded purpose that the air they expelled was put in service of during "The Great Misspeak." Let me say that if I know my lungs, they would never have cooperated were they aware of what lay ahead for the air they were soon to expel through my vocal cords.

This leads me to the big one: where was my brain in all of this? I'll tell you where it was: nowhere to be found. My heart is in pain because my brain had abstained. Hey, that rhymes. Anyhow, my brain really needs to "show up" for these events where my mouth is talking. I'm thinking of employing a "brain/mouth" rule if you choose me for Senate.

So let me be clear: I do not think that the words *rape*, *guilty*, and *pleasure* belong in the same sentence—or even paragraph. I probably shouldn't have used the word *retarded* earlier, either, but I am typing this and my fingers may yet be attempting an overthrow. Oh, if only you all could hear what my heart is thinking!

This, then, is my apology, and I hope it suffices. I have been asked to withdraw from the race by my party, my friends, my wife, and my conscience, but my gut won't let me.

I FOUND A JACKSON POLLOCK!

Excuse me for jumping and shouting "Hooray!"
But I found a Jackson Pollock today!
It was under the stairs, behind some chairs.
It had been there for years, we were all unawares.
In a spare space a-clutter with old brooms and dustbins,
in rurally rural old rural Wisconsin!

At first I'd no idea, unsure what I'd found,
some old thing worth nothing, thought I—
nothing world renowned…

But now I know it's a Pollock and here's how I know—
all the splotches of paint are placed there just so.
They "pop" and they mingle to coax forth a mood,
they tell you a story, they force you to brood,
upon their deep meaning, there's just something MORE there
than just splotches of paint that are going nowhere.
So I know it's a real one—
a top-notch big deal one—
the kind that will hang in a Met or a Getty,
and when I know what it's worth, will I sell it?
You bet-y!

But how will I prove it? There's no autograph,
I might show it to everyone and everyone will just laugh.
I have searched for a fingerprint or a hair I could test,
to prove that my Pollock is ol' Jack at his best.
I can't find a one, not a single damn follicle—
but I know if I did it would surely be Pollockle!
Oh, relax, I am certain, no need to get colicky,
the experts will swear that my Pollock is Pollocky.

So, what was it doing in Grandmama's storage?
Forgotten before I went out on my forage?
Let's just say Grandma wandered, she roved and she mingled,
before she was married, back when she was single.
Famous names, it was rumored, she'd befriend and be-met,
she was the toast of New York,
and the belle of 'gansett!
(A side note: my Pollock was swaddled in paper,
with typing upon it I've just begun to decipher.
Some absurdishy prose about night and its mother
signed by a Kurt Vonne-something-or-other.)

But if finders aren't keepers,
if that's not enough,
to prove provenance and stop all the guff—
listen here, final proof is coming your way,
and you won't put a roadblock in my big payday.
Grandma knew there'd be doubters, second-guessers, and pros
who would line up to back up each other's big "no's."

A line of art experts, a doubt promenade!
So she wrote very clearly for whom it was made—
In the corner the dedication: "Bobby O., 2nd Grade"!

Famous Quotations—Unabridged

"*Know Thyself.* Come on. Hurry up. We're waiting. Oh, forget it."

—Socrates

ABS

Y ou are probably wondering where I got these amazing abs. They're so ripply and rock hard, they're difficult to fathom. If I were a character on a reality show about me and my middle-aged acquaintances, I might be nicknamed the Conundrum, in reference to these abs of mine. See, the abs don't match the visage. My perturbed, puffy face sets you up for a blubbery gut. But then you see these abs, stacked like bricks, clearly delineated, and you have to ask, "Does he work out for two or three hours a day, or does he just work out all day?" Or perhaps you think I purchased them from a plastic surgeon in Beverly Hills. My secret is simple—dynamic tension! Constant dynamic tension. Tension that is tense, and dynamic, and never ending—the best kind of tension there is! I have analyzed each ab and where it draws its tension from so that you, too, can get the abs you've always dreamed of!

The ab on the upper right is taut and sinewy thanks to middle school. Specifically, the effort of trying to get my two kids placed in a top-notch middle school. Filling out forms, attending open houses, prepping for interviews, taking the entrance exams—it's a lot of work, and I am there every step of the way, standing behind them, leaning over their shoulders, looking down (that's what tightens the ab), swallowing hard (also good for the ab), and clenching and unclenching my fists (good for the fists). Thanks, kids—Dad loves you and Dad loves the ab you've given him.

The middle-right ab bulges handsomely thanks to talk radio. I simply tune in to conservative talkers when I am driving, and my screaming at the host tightens this ab for an extended, uninterrupted rep. Plus, disagreeing with someone on the radio gives me that powerless, overwhelmed feeling I've become addicted to. It's better than a drug, because you get the abs!

The upper-left ab pops out impressively from the effort of lugging five-gallon water jugs into our kitchen. Actually, the lugging does nothing for the ab; it's the part where you have to tip the full jug and place its spout into the dispensing reservoir, without spilling, that strains and sculpts this beautiful ab. The short moment of dread focuses tension on this ab like a ray gun. Afterward, slipping on the spilled water can be great for a whole-body clench.

The middle ab on the left (not my left, your left, if you are looking at me) is called Terrence. It's a dignified ab. It tenses each time I read an op-ed article about global warming. The article's point of view is immaterial; simply being reminded that I can do nothing to stop the horrific future of floods and catastrophe gives this ab a taut yank that lingers, burning calories in my well-creased forehead at the same time. Best to do right before bed, as the accompanying nightmares keep those abs pumping into the early-morning hours!

The bottom-right ab, the biggest of all the abs—and therefore the most impressive—is from not having sex. This ab is always quietly tensed. Has been for years now. Can you imagine the Dalai Lama's lower right ab? Must be huge. I, however, did not take a vow of chastity, so it would be a sad situation, if it didn't yield such an amazing ab.

The bottom ab on the left is harder to explain, but I believe that this ab is simply self-aware. It quivers with tension at all times, even more so when I am supposed to be relaxing, and I believe it is searching for a sense of purpose for itself and no answer is forthcoming. Nothing works this ab like a vacation. The aimless uncertainty, the absence of all deadlines, tightens and sculpts like nothing else. After ten days in Hawaii, this ab looks amazing.

Finally, you've got to appreciate my extra abs. That's right, I have two abs more than most people. They are in my lower back, and, I'll admit it, they were put there by my Beverly Hills plastic surgeon. I was told that they are the latest thing. God, I hope so. They hurt like hell.

Famous Quotations—Unabridged

—————➤◆◄—————

"*There is nothing on this earth more to be prized than true friendship,* but one of those heated bathroom floors? That comes close— real close."

—Thomas Aquinas

SHAKESPEARE IN THE PARK

EXT. PRISON
INT. PRISON MEETING ROOM
In a sad, generic meeting room, five prisoners sit in their faded orange jumpsuits, rough characters all. In this California federal prison, they are mostly Latino. A fellow prisoner strides in with heavy energy and a shredded face. His imposing size adds to a sense of his own gravity. He is Placidio, their Director, and he is the big dog in this pack—not to be messed with! They, the prisoners, are in a theater group. What else is there to do—it's prison!
Placidio unnecessarily silences the already silent group.

>   PLACIDIO
> Okay, motherfuckers, shut the hell up!
>   (*beat*)
> Now I want to congratulate you all on
> an excellent production of *Steamboat* last
> Friday. The reviews are in: you're the hit
> of the whole prison, but before you get
> swell heads, I want to tell you your prize:
> you have to take on Shakespeare!! The
> immortal Bard! Every prisoner's challenge:
> the language, the passions, the intellect!

No reaction from the assembled. They're not sure how to take this. Some smell a challenge. No one high-fives.

> PLACIDIO (CONT'D)
> Now, before you go high-fiving, because
> you were all so great in the last produc-
> tion, I'm going to let you pick which play
> you get to do.

> LUIS
> Uhhh, *any* Shakespeare play?

> PLACIDIO
> Any one at all. The challenge of a
> lifetime…you lifers!

> LUIS
> Well, I guess it's hard to choose. There's
> so many…

Suddenly, in the back of the room, ROBERT speaks up. Robert is a white-collar criminal, only here due to spillover at the "country club" prison up the road…

> ROBERT
> Placidio has issued us a challenge. I have
> not been the most vocal of inmates, but if
> you'll allow me to speak as a used-to-be
> patron of the arts, I'd say, if I had to vote,
> I'd vote for…Shakespeare in the Park.

The other prisoners aren't sure about Robert, but we can see his sugges-tion has an immediate attraction to them.

RAFALIO

Sounds good to me.

RANDALL

Yeah, I like that one best.

There is general agreement all around, but before this wildfire can catch wind, Placidio wants to clarify his intent...

PLACIDIO

Okay, well, maybe you don't understand
the question so good, but *which* of the
great Shakespeare's plays would you
choose to do?

ROBERT

I understood you perfectly—I am a
great aficionado of the Bard, and I would
propose we take on *In the Park*. That one.
Its full name is *Shakespeare in the Park*.

The other prisoners, who've never given a second look to Robert, are suddenly on his side in a big way. Their energy gathers in a restless mummering, but they silence when Placidio puts up his hand—

PLACIDIO

Wait, motherfuckers, wait! There's no
such thing, man. I don't think...

ROBERT

Uh, indeed there is. I saw it many years
ago. More than once. It was great. They
performed it outside, just as Shakespeare
intended!

*Rafalio, no friend of Robert's (he tried to kill Robert once...a day, for
the past four years), is suddenly on his enemy's side—*

RAFALIO

Yeah, I've heard of it. The best play ol'
Bill Shakespeare ever wrote.

EDDIE

I know it, too! *Shakespeare in the Park!*
They do it every year in my hometown.
New York.

Placidio hesitates, he is not on firm footing here—

PLACIDIO

Okay, slow down, look...you mean, you
saw a Shakespeare *play*, like *Othello*, or
Richard the Third, or *Hamlet*...IN THE
PARK. Right? Yeah?

LUIS

I don't know about that...it was just
called *Shakespeare in the Park* when
I saw it.

Charlie, thirty-four and obese, with fine features and extensive facial tattoos, completely out of his league, suddenly butts in—

CHARLIE
(*growing more sure of himself as he speaks*)
Yeah, me too…I saw that play, too. Yeah.
I loved it. I love Shakespeare, all of him,
but this one…yes, is his best.

LUIS
Yeah, man, it had everything.

PLACIDIO
Like what, then? What happens in it?

LUIS
Well, this kid slept with his mother, the
queen…

PLACIDIO
That's *Hamlet*…

RAFALIO
Oh, yeah, and then this Dad-King killed
his sons…

PLACIDIO
Richard the Third…

CHARLIE
…then at the end, the sprite from the

Garden told them all the moral!

PLACIDIO
Well, that's *Midsummer Night's Dream*,
man! You got it wrong—

LUIS
No, YOU got it wrong—it's
Shakespeare's greatest play: *In the Park*!
It's what we want and we won't settle for
anything less…right, guys?!

All the prisoners start pounding on their desks…

PRISONERS
In the Park…In the Park…In the Park!

*The Director, scarier than the rest of the inmates, begins to back off—
a riot is about to begin! Suddenly the door opens and a GUARD and
WARDEN DANIELS enter.*

WARDEN DANIELS
What the hell? Quiet down! All of you!

The Guard waves his gun and the prisoners quiet down.

WARDEN DANIELS (CONT'D)
The heck is going on in here, Placidio?

PLACIDIO
These motherfuckers, they can't decide which
play they want to do for the next round.

LUIS

We did decide! We want to do
SHAKESPEARE IN THE PARK!

The prisoners cheer, but the Warden is skeptical, until—

ROBERT

Placidio said it was our choice and we
choose *Shakespeare in the Park*—what's
wrong with that? I love that play, it's
dear to me, it's dear to all of us, it's got
everything: romance, betrayal, fresh air,
sunlight! It's the Bard's most rewarding
entertainment yet!

Warden Daniels takes this in, then remembers he doesn't give a shit.

WARDEN DANIELS

Oh...well, go ahead. It's one of my
favorites.

The prisoners cheer and hug each other!

WARDEN DANIELS (CONT'D)

But I'm warning you! It's not taking
place in some fake park here in the
prison; if we do it, we do it in a real
park, outside! Theater is already so
fakey, it makes me sick. I want to *feel*
something—you got me?! Make me see
eternity!

The prisoners nod…hell, yeah. As they celebrate, Placidio throws his hands up in the air—what has he wrought? And we hear the narrator answer his query…

> NARRATOR (V.O.)
> All of Cell Block Three escaped
> during the first on-site rehearsal of the
> production.
> (*beat*)
> But their understudies from Cell Block
> Five went on in their place and made
> theater history.

WHAT TO DO IN CASE OF FIRE

I n case of fire, do not panic: the historic Dubonot Hotel, aka "The Piano Hotel," built in 1914, will be fine. Over its storied history, the historic Dubonot—"The Hotel with a Player Piano in the Lobby"—has played host to more than 275 (reported) fires— and just look at it! Look around you! The old gal is fine. Some plaster is missing, sure, but we can replace that, and we will, we will. Basically, these kinds of things happen to this hotel all of the time.

Why so many fires? This is probably due to the fact that the historic "Dubonot: the Hotel with the Indefatigable Music Machine" was built directly over a little-known natural-gas fissure in San Francisco's bedrock. One side effect of this constant seepage of natural gas is the delectable aroma of raw eggs wafting about every nook and cranny. In 1989, Chef Jeremy of Pierre's, our in-house restaurant, decided to turn a negative into a positive and set out to make the best omelets in the city. He has succeeded spectacularly and is listed in the *Guinness Book of World Records* for "cracking the most eggs per year" and for "surviving the most kitchen fires of any chef, ever" (229 fires).

Built in 1916, the historic Dubonot is not, as rumor has it, "always" on fire. It is, more aptly put, "usually" on fire. Another word that springs to mind is *oftentimes*. Our "famous" lobby has had a continuously playing player piano since 1969, and only eighty-seven of the fires have ever burned it down completely. Seventy-eight fires were put out before making it to the lobby, one hundred and thirty-seven of our fires were kept to the basement level, and only fifty-six fires were determined enough to destroy the player piano itself. Mysteriously, one hundred and eighty-seven fires that were started by arson were started near or within the piano itself—as though in retribution for its neverending merrymaking.

While a fire engulfs the Historic Dubonot Hotel, please avoid the elevators and use the stairs.

THE SECOND MEETING OF
JESUS AND LAZARUS

E verybody knows the story of how Jesus raised Lazarus from the dead.

Except you. You forgot. The details. The "deets." Sheesh. Okay, here goes...

It seems Lazarus, the brother of Mary from Bethany, had fallen sick, deeply sick, in the way people living in the desert at that time did. This was only a short while after Jesus left town—he'd been there "teaching" and being worshipped. Laz's sister had actually washed Jesus' feet. Nice. Anyway, Jesus was on his general roving "mission" when his sixth sense got to tingling. He knew he had to return. But get this: by the time he got back, Lazarus had been in the tomb for four days, so he was good and dead. Now, that didn't stop Jesus, who marched right into the tomb alone and came out with Lazarus right beside him, whistling and winking all the way. Okay, I'm not sure he was whistling and winking, but I'll bet he felt like doing both. After all, Lazarus had been dead, and now he wasn't. An "exponential qualitative change," if ever there was such a thing.

So that's the nutshell of it all, but hold up—this wasn't the only time Jesus and Lazarus had a face-to-face. A few months later, they met again. Jesus was outside a temple trying to look inconspicuous, taking a break from messiah-ing, and Lazarus traveled for a day and three nights—one day he was sidetracked due to the heat, and finally he arrived at the J-man's vicinity and ran right up to him, breathless, to thank him and ask a few questions...

I think it might have gone like this.

[*To be read aloud to yourself in the voice of Bob Newhart.*]

Jesus! Hey, Jesus! Hi...hey...it's me.

What do you mean you don't remember me? You helped me.

No, I'm sure you DO help "a lot of people." But I think you'll remember me—I mean, you REALLY helped me.

I'm Lazarus! The dead guy! You made me alive again! Yeah, *that* Lazarus! Right. Yeah, so...I wanted to say "thank you" and...if you don't mind, ask a question or two. Yeah? Okay, well. First, in case you're wondering, I'm fine. Lovin' life, TCB and all that—I mean, my foot fell asleep last week, and that gave me a scare, but I just shook it around and everything's fine. (*chuckles*)

Yeah, my question...well, my question is simply this: am I *ever* going to die?

I will. I'll die...*again?* Wow, you seem pretty sure—you spoke pretty quick there. Sure, I believe you, I just...I guess the follow-up to that, then, would be...where and when and...how will I die...*again.* [*awkward laugh*]

You know but won't say? Yeah, I figured you might have that kind of rule. I guess you'd have everybody badgering you if you didn't. Fair enough, but, uh...just one more thing, if I DO die again, I mean, WHEN I die a *second* time, will you be…stopping by to…bring me back from the dead again? Or, was that a one-time deal?

One-time only. Got it.

Are you sure?

"Pretty sure." Like, how sure? Is there a twenty percent chance that you would raise me up again? Fifteen? No? Ten? Three? Less than three percent? *No* chance. Okay. Wow. That's…

No, I understand. I'm not disappointed, per se…I may not *want* to keep coming back to life, but…what if I ask? I mean, what if I *asked* you to raise me from the dead, you know, as I'm dying?

Still a no. Wow, you're pretty committed to this. Okay. I mean—it seems a bit unfair. Just, I already died once, it wasn't pleasant, now I *get* to do it again. I'm not complaining, but…

What's that? If I believe in you I will live forever? So, then I won't die?

Oh, so you're saying "figuratively" I will live…in some heaven, somewhere? What's that like? What happens there?

So it's sort of a limbo place where everyone sings your praises all day and night? Hmm…yeah, well, no, I get why *you* think it's a pretty great place. It sounds…

My dead relatives will all be there? Are you trying to make it sound *less* attractive? Anyway, thanks again for…you know— *that one time*, and I guess I'll see you around, 'kay?

[*LAZARUS walks away, thoughtful, but gets only a short way before he turns around and runs up to Jesus with a big grin on his face—*]

Hold up a second—I get what you're doing here! Last time I died I was dead for four days before you raised me up! You wanted me to think it was going to go on forever! Then you popped in and Boom! I'm up! What are you going to do this time? Make me wait *five* days? Tssss… You're prankin' me! You're hustling my ass!

Oh—you really mean it, you're NOT going to raise me up again? I don't believe you, man…I can see your smile—you don't fool me. Nice one…nice try.

[*LAZARUS winks and walks away, nodding his head and grinning. Jesus stares at the ground, shaking his head.*]

ACTUAL-FACTUAL NEW
JESUS FACTS

A fresh new Dead Sea Scroll was discovered and deciphered last year, and some fascinating facts about the historical figure of Jesus have come to light.

1. Jesus Christ went by the name Jesus and was only called "Geez" by his closest friends.
2. He NEVER used the name Jesus H. Christ as we know it. However, there are documents signed "Holy Christ" and "Christ Almighty." There is no record of him appearing under the moniker "Jesus Christ Almighty" or "Gee Whiz."
3. He once hosted a comedy-benefit-revue-style show for lepers where he appeared in drag as "Geez Louise."

Famous Quotations—Unabridged

⟫•⟪

"*A girl should be two things: classy and fabulous.* Oh, and shallow—really, really shallow."

—Coco Chanel

SO YOU WANT TO GET
A TATTOO!

"A tattoo is forever." —Steven Hawkings*

FIRST, PAUSE!

It's true: a tattoo, drawn in permanent ink, will stay on your body forever, so you need to make the RIGHT CHOICE. You need time to think about the possibilities, contemplate what has meaning for you, and consider how the image will age with you in time. With this in mind, we have the three criteria you should follow for tattoo hunting:

1.   Do Not Be in a Hurry.
2.   Do Not Be Drunk.
3.   Do Not Be Drunk and in a Hurry.

These are simple directives, but if you cannot follow them, we understand. It's very common for these simple rules to be discarded in the face of the notion of getting a permanent tattoo permanently drilled into your skin forever and ever.

---

* Not Steven Hawking, the other guy—I'm talking about the fat one who says obvious things.

So, you're set on it, are you? You are getting a tattoo, and you're drunk, and you have to do it right now? Fine. Glad I made that first list. Onward.

MAKE A LIST OF THINGS YOU LOVE!

You need to make a list of things you love. These cannot be things you love today, or this week, or even this year. These must be things you've loved for a long, long time. Below is an example list. This is not necessarily the list you would make, but it's close enough so that you can use it, since you're drunk and in a hurry.

Example Tattoo List:
1. Mom (yours)
2. Favorite movie (e.g., *The Big Lebowski*)
3. Girlfriend's name (e.g., "Jane")
4. Favorite rock band (e.g., "RUSH")
5. Favorite album/year (e.g., *2112*)
6. Celtic/yin-yang design
7. Something you like, have always liked, and will always like (e.g., "A Piece of Chocolate Cake")

Let's look closer at your list.

First of all, "Mom," the classic, made popular by men who'd spent time in the trenches of WWI and its sequel, *WWII: Germany Doubles Down*. These men made wise choices, getting tattoos that reminded them of their mothers—the only women who truly loved them. Keep in mind, this was the early part of last century, so these were stay-at-home moms. Nowadays Mom has to work to keep the family in two cars and wireless devices (and a house), so we justifiably feel far less affection for her. Scratch Mom off the list.

The second one—favorite movie. Here you might choose to get the name of the movie tattooed, or a character—like the popular character of the Dude from *The Big Lebowski*. This will always remind you of a lazy stoner guy who made you smile whenever he was on screen. Here's the rub; if you get this tattoo, then people will always be playing this movie for you—at every birthday, at your bachelor (or bachelorette) party, on Father's Day. No movie can withstand this kind of scrutiny, believe me. I know a guy with an image of *Napoleon Dynamite* on his forearm and he's constantly asked if he "still loves that movie," to which he always grins and says, "Leave me alone."

This same logic can be applied to the next two tattoo possibilities on your list: you favorite rock band and/or album. Your taste will change as you grow older. You may even stop listening to music completely as you turn fifty and become enamored of talk radio and the rantings of your favorite pundit, or when your "favorite" band reunites for "one last tour" and you pay too much to see them and they just sound like crap, and Neal Peart looks like the angry neighbor who called the cops on you when you were a teenager. I promise you will get sick of your favorite music right now, no matter how much you like it. However, you can always get a tattoo of "Weird Al" Yankovic, as he's a "perennial"—and thanks to his ironic dimension, he remains relevant forever.

Do not get a Celtic symbol or a yin-yang design. They just

become wallpaper. People won't even ask you about them. What good is a tattoo if it evokes nothing from people around you? It has to be a statement of some kind. You're not *that* drunk, are you?

Finally, something you love, always have, and always will. "A Piece of Chocolate Cake." Is this a legit tattoo? I've never seen it done, but here's what I know. Everyone likes chocolate, and everyone likes cake. People like chocolate cake even if they've *just finished eating* a piece of chocolate cake. Children like it, alienated teenagers like it, and old people love it. Wherever you are, people will see your tattoo and immediately feel connected to you! Every time you look in the mirror and see it, you will ask yourself, "Why did I get this? Oh, right—I LOVE chocolate cake! I should get a piece right now! Thanks, tattoo!"

So, it's settled then. You are getting a tattoo of either "Weird Al" Yankovic or the words A PIECE OF CHOCOLATE CAKE. (Between you and me, I hope you'll get the cake one—it'll make me laugh.)

A VISION OF THE FUTURE

I t's the year 3012 and all food is gluten-free. No restaurant, grocery, or bakery serves anything with gluten in it, and guess what? Everything still tastes great. But that's not the only thing that's changed.

The amount of time people save by not having to ask—or answer—the question "Is that gluten-free?" when ordering food has lengthened every individual's life span by an estimated fourteen hours. This "extra time" is used by most people to write negative reviews on the Internet of things they see or hear or have heard about.

Cars run on gluten-free fuel, which is an improvement on the green fuel that replaced gasoline completely in 2567. The original green fuel was a combination of wheat, seaweed, and curry powder. It was loaded with gluten, and then there was the fact that everything smelled like curry. I mean *everything*—the whole of *outdoors*—curry.

A race war is raging. Latinos and Asians are kicking butt. Blacks and whites are losing. Lots of deaths, but thankfully, it didn't impede the effort to reduce the amount of gluten in food.

Jerusalem is at peace. Israel is back to its 1967 borders, and the Palestinians and Israelis are best friends. Interesting fact: there are more bar mitzvahs performed in Palestine than anywhere else on earth. At these bar mitzvahs, only gluten-free food is served—but you knew that already.

In 2997, the scientist Dontaurius Morgan finally figured out how to remove all gluten from food without losing flavor or consistency. He had a full career as a footballer, playing halfback for the Liverpool Beatles team for the maximum eight concussions. He then attended Harvard-on-the-Moon University, a division of the University of Phoenix, the world's most respected institution of higher learning. Statues of Dontaurius are all over the place. It's considered good luck to rub the statue's belly and pinch its nipples. This is kinda weird, but...what can you do?

A spaceship called the Starship *Enterprise* has been traveling through space for nearly a hundred years, exacerbating conflicts and instigating quarrels. Experts suspect that the crew is attempting to reintroduce gluten into the food supply.

People live to be 130 years old on average—and they live well. My wife can eat anything, anywhere, without calling ahead to check on what they serve, or if it's gluten-free. We go out a lot, so, yeah, life is pretty great. Except for the horrible, rampant racism.

OBIT FOR THE CREATOR
OF MAD LIBS

On Tuesday, in Canton, Connecticut, a town famous for the *stickiness* of its *boogers*, a *stinky* old man died of a *good* disease at his home at 345 *Rotten* Lane. Mr. Preston Wirtz, whose parents, *Ida and Goober*, ran a small *jelly* farm, died in his *yellowish toilet*. Mr. Wirtz was *hated* in *Uzbekistan* for the series of word-play books he created for *slippery* children, books known far and wide as "Mad Libs," beloved by *hairy grumps* and *farty grampas* alike. These books were *never* appreciated by *tall elves*, selling over *two* per year for *one decade*. When asked to describe Mr. Wirtz, his *jealous* wife, wearing nothing but an *egg carton* and *flip-flops*, called him "in a nutshell, the most *sour-smelling, bacon-licking, pimple-footed crab-apple* I have ever known. I will *never always* miss him and his *broken underwear*." Then she cried herself to sleep in her *fart-house*.

Famous Quotations—Unabridged

—————➤➤•◄◄—————

"*It's the job that's never started as takes longest to finish.* But that's
nothing compared to writing a trilogy—that takes fucking forever."

—J. R. R. Tolkien

THAT'S QUITE ENOUGH OF
YOU, ODENKIRK

A half a damn century of me. Enough.
     I am deeply thankful that I have slipped past death's
hinky radar so far. If he ever caught sight of my sorry ass, the
Reaper would surely label me a "waste of space," whip out his
scythe, and mutter, in a tight close-up, "I *live* for this shit." Then
he'd cackle in surround sound, swoop through a time hole, and
take me down as I walked unsuspectingly through a busy intersec-
tion in LA reading a British tabloid on my smartphone. And hell,
I'd deserve it, wouldn't I?

I already told my kids: when I die, no parades. No parades
and no holiday, either. Keep it simple. I just want a simple statue.
A simple, life-size statue, to scale—except in the crotch. Give yer
pops a boost there for old times' sake, and mount that statue on a
simple granite base in the foyer of the White House. That's all.
Because I'd like to be remembered as just another great American
with a slightly larger-than-normal-sized endowment in the crotch,
thank you very much.

People whom I haven't seen in a while come up to me and
say, in a tone of upbeat surprise, "Bob, is that you? Wow, you
look great!" And it doesn't come across as a compliment, because
I look "okay," just okay. So then I have to wonder: how old, tired,

bald, and paunchy did you think I would be by now? Did you think that the next time you saw me I would be a sagging, flabby, hairy sweatball you could hardly recognize if my personal nurse didn't tell you who I used to be? What do you think I'm doing when you aren't seeing me standing right in front of you? Sitting in the sun eating burgers, drinking beer, listening to soft rock, and melting? I got a life, dammit! Give me some credit.

OTHER BOOKS BY THIS AUTHOR

SO YOU WANT TO WRITE A BOOK?

In this masterpiece of the how-to genre, Bob Odenkirk asks his readers questions such as *You want to write a book? Really? Why? Wasn't this one good enough for you? What about the other twenty billion books you can pick up for free at the library? Oh, I get it, none of them contain* your *life story. Are you sure? Have you checked? Double-check.*

CATALOG OF MY FEELINGS

A list—literally *a list*—of the author's feelings. Not numbered. Neither in alphabetical nor chronological order. No commentary is made, no specifics are given, nothing concrete is described. Set a world record for "most uses of the word *angry* in a book." Fascinating.

HOW TO RECYCLE PAPER

A twelve-pound book printed on 100 percent recycled heavyweight card-stock paper. Achieves its aim.

Inspired by *Monty Python*, *Bob and Ray*, and shows he'd seen at Chicago's Second City Theatre, Bob started writing sketches for his classes in junior high. He went on to write for *Saturday Night Live* (where he wrote the "Motivational Speaker" sketch), and *The Ben Stiller Show* (where he wrote the infamous "Manson Lassie" sketch). Bob went on to create (and star in) *Mr. Show with Bob and David*, which has been called "the American Monty Python." He goosed along the creation of *Tim and Eric Awesome Show, Great Job!* on Adult Swim and was a key element in the birth of *The Birthday Boys* on IFC.

As an actor, Bob has had memorable roles as the agent Stevie Grant on *The Larry Sanders Show*, the character of Saul Goodman on AMC's *Breaking Bad*, as well as in Alexander Payne's Oscar-nominated film *Nebraska*. He will reprise his *Breaking Bad* role in *Better Call Saul*, a new spin-off series on AMC.

Bob's comedy scripts and short essays have appeared in the *New Yorker*, *VICE*, *Filter*, and elsewhere.

ACKNOWLEDGMENTS

I'd like to thank Mike Sacks for coaxing me on, Dave Eggers for making it come to life, Andrew Leland and Dan McKinley for making it look sharp, and Sharon Alagna for taking my author photo. Miss Sally Pemberton's introduction was graciously provided by Megan Amram. Cover and interior illustrations are by Tony Millionaire. *Proud Gay Grampa* comic was illustrated by Scott C. "Didn't Work for Me," "Portrait of the Artist," "A Vision of the Future," and "Where I Got These Abs" originally appeared in the *New Yorker* (or at newyorker.com) in slightly different form. Lastly, thanks to the Directors and Members of the LilyGuild NY Local 214, without whose support this work would not have been possible.